ART
EXPRESS
BOOK 4

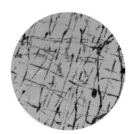

EILEEN ADAMS

ROSEMARY BIGNELL

JANE BOWER

JUDY GRAHAME

MICHÈLE CLAIRE KITTO

KEVIN MATHIESON

DON

First published 2009
By A&C Black Publishers Ltd
36 Soho Square, London W1D 3QY
© 2009 A&C Black Publishers Ltd
ISBN 978 0 7136 8481 0 (Book & CD-ROM)
ISBN 978 1 4081 2222 8 (Site licence)

Unit text, and photographs unless otherwise stated © Eileen Adams (drawing); Rosemary Bignell (sculpture); Jane Bower (printing); Judy Grahame (painting); Michèle Claire Kitto (collage); Kevin Mathieson (digital technology)

CREDITS

Series Editor: *Julia Stanton*
Series Designer: *Elizabeth Healey*
Resource Sheet Designer: *Christina Newman (Black Dog Design)*
Editors: *Tanya Solomons, Monica Byles*
Picture Researchers: *Holly Beaumont, Emma Brown*
Illustrations: *Celia Hart*
CD-ROM Programming: *Q&D Ltd*
Publisher: *Linda Lambert*

ACKNOWLEDGEMENTS

The publishers would like to thank the following teachers who reviewed the material in their schools: Katie Epps and Laurence Keel. Also, the Editorial Board for their support during the project: Dan China, Jane Bower and Judy Grahame. The authors would like to thank the following schools for their help in facilitating the photographs used in the book.

Drawing: For permission to use images from schools in Swansea and Carmarthenshire, Wales, involved in the *My Square Mile* Project, grateful thanks to Lynne Bebb, Carolyn Davies and Sophie Hadaway; Art and the *Built Environment* Project archive; The Campaign for Drawing; Gill Figg; the *Josef Herman* Project; Zek Hoeben; Lincolnshire School Improvement Service; Sorai Nicolson; Batley Parish C of E School, Batley, West Yorks.; Eveline Lowe Primary School, Southwark, London; Kilburn Park Primary School, London; Overton Primary School, Greenock, Scotland. **Painting**: Somerhill Junior School, Hove, Brighton and Hove. **Printing**: Peterborough High School, Junior Dept., Cambs.; Fiona Sakol, Kings College School, Cambridge. **Collage & Textiles**: Abingdon Preparatory School, Oxon.; St Aloysius' Catholic Primary School, Oxford; The Oratory Prep School, Reading, Berks.; Dr South's C of E Primary School, Islip, Oxon. **Sculpture**: Deptford Park Primary School and Kender Primary School, both in Lewisham, London. **Digital media**: Parklee Community School; Hindsford School; St George's School, all in Atherton, London.

The rights of the authors of this work have been asserted by them in accordance with the Copyright, Designs and Patents Act 1988.

A CIP catalogue record for this book is available from the British Library.

CONTENTS

ABOUT ART EXPRESS

Art Express was developed at a time of change. It builds upon the first national curriculum which established the underlying principles, content and practice of art education. However, it allows schools to take ownership of their own curriculum content and to tailor it for their specific needs. *Art Express* illustrates how high-quality subject teaching can still be used to underwrite the development and evolution of new curriculum practice and supports teachers' professional development. Core to this approach are the role of new media, the significance of cross-curricular areas of learning and the importance of drawing as a key element of learning. The series covers the primary concepts and key processes of art education via six content areas –

- **Drawing**
- **Painting**
- **Printing**
- **Collage & Textiles**
- **Sculpture**
- **Digital Media**

Philosophy

Art Express is underwritten by clear principles about the nature and role of art in education. Central to this lies the understanding of art education as a process of generating ideas, realising them in material form, and being able to talk about what was done and why. This is best expressed as a set of three principles underlying each unit and session. They are seen clearly in the consistent pattern of learning objectives and assessment outcomes. Such principles are not unique to art education, and teachers will recognise the broader areas of learning and the duties on school to prepare pupils for the experiences of later life.

The three principles are related to:

- The development of ideas and creativity
- The development of skills and mastery of processes
- The development of knowledge encompassing art and cultures.

Art and Education

Art Express takes a broad view of education and the role that art can play. Its principles echo across the curriculum. They indicate how art can contribute to essential aspects of children's personal development such as creativity, independence, judgement and self-reflection.

Art Express includes regular opportunities to learn about and explore other cultures: celebrating different cultural traditions while avoiding outdated stereotypes that should no longer have a place in children's understanding of our multicultural world.

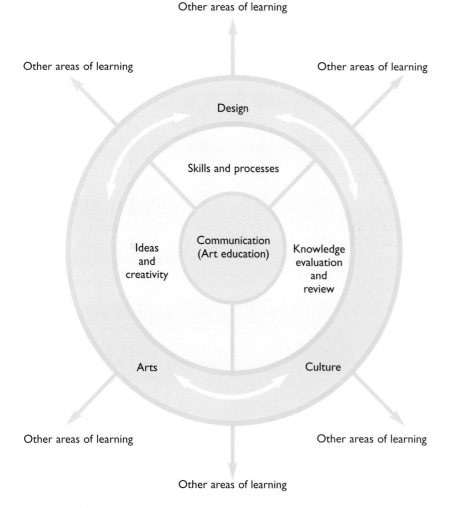

Other areas of learning

Other areas of learning

Other areas of learning

Design

Skills and processes

Ideas and creativity

Communication (Art education)

Knowledge evaluation and review

Arts

Culture

Other areas of learning

Other areas of learning

Other areas of learning

IN THE CLASSROOM

Teaching

The units in *Art Express* exemplify good practice in teaching. They are written to model progression from first-hand experimentation and the acquisition of skills and technical knowledge, towards applying what has been learned with new independence and purpose, enabling pupils to become self-aware and confident learners.

Planning

The *Art Express* units have sequential logic and may be used as a scheme of work. The units build upon prior learning – progression and continuity are built into the scheme. The programme for each year ensures that the breadth and balance of experience, skills and curriculum content is appropriate for the age range.

However, from the outset, the editorial board of *Art Express* has been anxious to create a model of practice that is open to change and modification by creative teachers. Teachers will find it easy to adapt units to fit in with local circumstances and curriculum. For instance, all units may be adapted for different age ranges, purposes and contexts.

Within *Art Express*, the units illustrate how planned learning is sequential and cumulative. They model the process of enquiry and experimentation that generates ideas and develops familiarity with materials. This in turn promotes purposeful ideas and plans, following these through, mastering skills and regular reviewing of progress.

Each unit contains a sequence of sessions. These are not necessarily lessons of a fixed length but separate learning segments. For instance, some of the sessions in the digital media units are a series of short episodes, each of which must be completed before moving on. Teachers can manage these in different ways – for example, by using small groups or by adapting material from one session to cover several weeks. Alternatively, an arts week could compress sessions within a short time-frame, possibly held across the school, with activities for each year group structured from their appropriate book.

Assessment

Art Express provides a good model for assessment of learning. It offers examples of what teachers should observe children do to confirm that they have made anticipated gains in learning. Units often plan explicitly for children to discuss their findings, especially via the plenary. This offers the opportunity to assess children's comprehension and to review the next steps. It also reinforces the expectation for children to become partners in the assessment of their own progress, and thus to become more independent learners.

Art Express supports the increasing emphasis upon personalised learning by giving practical suggestions for managing issues such as differentiation in addition to reflection opportunities and self-assessment rubrics.

WHAT'S IN THE BOOKS

Each unit has an introduction page with key issues and aims for the topic. Double-page spreads contain full instructions for carrying out each session, including learning objectives and assessment for learning. Other areas of learning (right) offers ideas for extending the topic across the curriculum. Images on session pages (below) show examples of work from children who have trialled each project.

UNITS

The units in *Art Express* illustrate teaching and learning within six areas of experience – Painting, Printing, Sculpture, Collage & Textiles, Drawing and Digital Media. The first four units support learning through the progressive development of experience, skills and knowledge.

Drawing is seen as a key skill that underwrites all activity in art, and most units include it as ideas and plans are developed and revised. The drawing units themselves provide a complementary approach and can often be used in conjunction with other units. As stand-alone units, they focus on drawing as a means of perception, invention and communication and involve drawing from observation, memory and imagination.

Similarly, the digital media units have a dual role, in that the techniques and processes can be adapted and incorporated directly into the other units as part of exploring and developing ideas. Most of the digital media units seek to engage children directly with some first-hand experience of materials, and outcomes are often a combination of digital plus practical skills and techniques and demonstrate how digital media may be used creatively to support learning through art.

The units of work have been developed to support good practice in planning and assessment and in challenging children to reach high standards and to use their creativity and imagination. They also provide clear and practical advice and guidance on teaching the skills and techniques that children will need to master in order to achieve success.

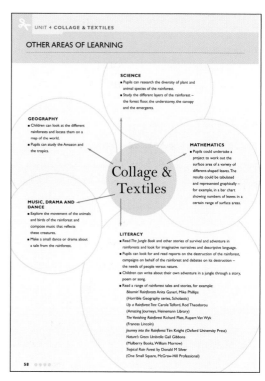

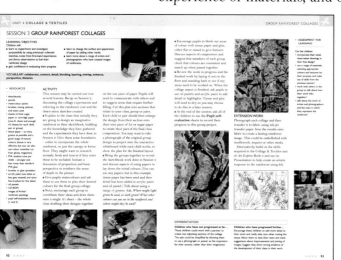

WHAT'S ON THE CD-ROM

The following supporting materials are available on the CD-ROM:

- Resource sheets – photocopiable and whiteboard resources for pupils and teachers
- Teacher assessment sheet per unit
- Pupil self-evaluation sheet per unit
- *PowerPoint* presentations
- Image library of Artists' works
- Library of reference images
- Image library of Children's work from trial schools
- *Chhau* dance drama stimulus video
- Virtual gallery with specially commissioned software to allow uploading of pupils' work
- Teachers reference including 'Skills and Processes' chart, list of suppliers and session-by-session unit vocabulary and resources.

RESOURCES

Art Express provides a range of further resources for teachers and children on the complementary CD-ROM. Teachers will find these resources inspire learning by presenting exciting visual examples and references. These resources are starting-points, examples and signposts – teachers will find many more resources locally and will adapt these to expand the collection.

Children will benefit from viewing large, bright images of art, crafts and

design on screen from disks or the internet. Where possible, teachers should also lead their pupils to first-hand experience of real arts, bringing artefacts into the classroom and organising outings to local art galleries and museums.

Finally, the CD-ROM contains an interactive **Virtual Gallery** – specially created software that will enable children to build their own art galleries to support reflection and discussion, and to celebrate the individual work of the school.

Above and left
Image library, including images of children's work.

Left
PowerPoint presentations include information and demonstrations for teachers and pupils.

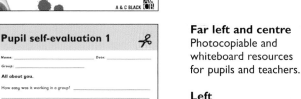

Far left and centre
Photocopiable and whiteboard resources for pupils and teachers.

Left
Pupil self-evaluation and teacher assessment sheets support each unit.

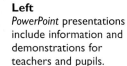

HOW TO USE THE CD-ROM

GETTING STARTED
- **PC**: the *Art Express* programme should auto-run when you insert the CD-ROM. If not, use My Computer to browse the contents of the CD-ROM and click on the File setup.
- **Mac**: insert the CD-ROM and double-click the *Art Express* icon. Open the folder and double-click the *Art Express* icon inside.

NETWORKING
Schools that have purchased a site licence are permitted to install and save the CD-ROM on a server and allow access on workstations within the school. Out-of-school access is not permitted, and image download permissions remain as above.

Use the MSI installer to deploy *Art Express* if you have a suitable network, or install *Art Express* to a server using the method described in Getting Started. Then, at each workstation, browse to the Installation folder on the server and run the File setup. Follow the instructions to create a shortcut to *Art Express* on the workstation.

TECHNICAL SUPPORT
Email A&C Black Customer Services on educationalsales@acblack.com.

MINIMUM SPECIFICATION
- PC with CD-ROM drive: Windows 98, 2000, XP or Vista
- Processor: Pentium 2 (or equivalent), 1GHz
- Ram: 256 MB
- Graphics: 800 x 600, 16-bit display, 3D accelerator (recommended)
- Mac with CD-ROM drive: OS X 10.1.5 and above
- Processor: G4 1GHz
- Ram: 256 MB
- Graphics: 800 x 600, 16-bit display,
- 3D accelerator (recommended)

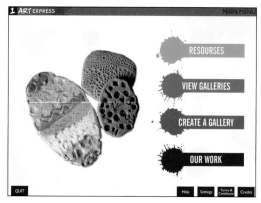

CD-ROM NAVIGATION
Main menu
From the main menu, teachers can access each of the following areas of the CD:

1. Teacher Resources
Access the bank of artist's and children's work, photos and videos, plus PDF and PowerPoint resources. Also view the artwork that you import from other sources.

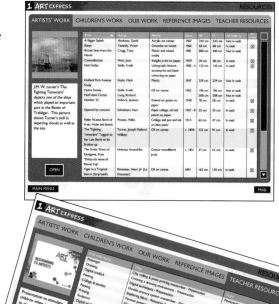

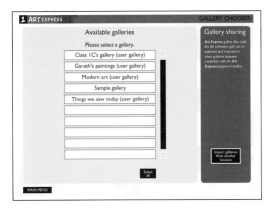

Image library of Artists' work
These are specific images referred to in the sessions; some may be imported into the **Virtual Gallery**, but not all.
Note: None of these images can be printed due to copyright provisions.

Library of reference images
These are additional images which may be referred to during sessions, or be used for reference or stimulus.

Image library of Children's work
These are images of work created by children during the trialling of the units in schools.

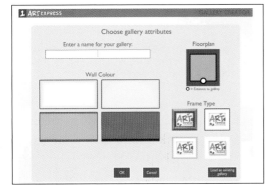

2. View Galleries
View the default virtual 3D galleries, together with the ones that you create. In this book there is only one pre-set gallery.

3. Create a Gallery
Use this to create your own virtual 3D gallery. Choose your floorplan, wall colour and framing theme, then get artist's work from the vault – or your own imported artwork – and position the pieces on the walls.

4. Our work
Use this to import image files into the programme to use in a virtual gallery or transfer them to another computer with *Art Express* installed.

1. Teacher Resources Menu
Once in the Teacher Resources menu, the following resources are accessed:

a) Images
There are three types of images available on the CD-ROM:

b) Resource sheets
Photocopiable and whiteboard resources for pupils and teachers.

c) Assessment sheets
Pupil self-evaluation and teacher assessment sheets support each unit.

d) Presentations
PowerPoint presentations for teachers and pupils, and masterclasses for teachers, which can be shared with pupils. (To alter or adapt the *PowerPoint* files, use these files stored in the folder on the CD-ROM.)

e) Video
Stimulus video for Ramayana.

f) Teachers' planning
Includes a 'Skills and Processes' chart for longterm planning, a list of suppliers and session-by-session vocabulary for each unit.

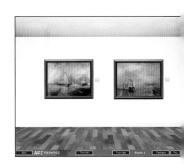

DRAWING IS DIFFERENT

Art Express supports contemporary curriculum modelling and planning as well as providing detailed guidance and support for teaching. The units of work have been developed to support good practice in planning, assessment and challenging pupils to reach high standards and to use their creativity and imagination. They also provide clear and practical guidance on teaching the skills and techniques that children will need to master in order to achieve success.

Foundation skill

In *Art Express*, drawing is seen as a core skill that underpins all activity in art. Indeed, as ideas and plans are developed and revised, most units will indicate the significant role of drawing via perception, invention and communication.

The drawing units themselves bear witness to the philosophy that sees the production of drawing as an internal dialogue for making choices, judgements and decisions – via observation, memory and imagination. The development of this internal communication strategy runs through every activity and each unit.

Technique and development

In learning to draw, children will gain experience of a wide range of tools and materials. They will develop a range of strategies and learn how drawing can be used for different purposes. However, teachers are invited to see drawing not purely as a set of techniques, but as a process that has much to do with attitude, habit, the ability to make connections and, above all, to be creative.

Expert author

The drawing units have been written by Eileen Adams who initiated the Campaign for Drawing programme, which resulted in the Big Draw, and numerous publications that explore the role of drawing as an essential and intrinsic part of learning and as a strategy for thinking.

Cross-curricular application

The drawing units are presented in a similar way to the other units, but teachers should use the activities and techniques as means of enriching and extending thinking and learning – across the curriculum wherever children are invited to think, look, speculate, imagine and come up with fresh ideas.

These activities are presented for use with particular age ranges and can be followed sequentially to provide a rich and intensive experience of drawing. Creative teachers, however, will also see opportunities to use these ideas for lessons in other sequences, with other age ranges and in a variety of curriculum situations.

For more information about the Campaign for Drawing and the work of Eileen Adams, go to: www.campaignfordrawing.org/ education/index.aspx

Drawing has been used throughout history to represent the world and make meaning – it is an important means of thinking. It is not only making marks on paper to represent things; it is also understanding experience and ideas, and sharing that knowledge. Children draw to explore their world, to understand it and to communicate their ideas to others. Drawing creates a sense of engagement; a personal and emotional response.

Prior to Year 4, pupils will have had many opportunities to draw using different materials, and they will have found pleasure in trying new things and experimenting. They should be accustomed to reflecting on their experience – talking about their progress and how they learn best. They should also be able to distinguish between different kinds of drawing and understand how drawing helps them communicate ideas, develop their thinking and resolve problems. Year 4 is perhaps a time to take stock and identify the range of purposes for which children use drawing, and to clarify the techniques used.

The drawing units in *Art Express* focus on learning through drawing using five themes – place, nature, buildings, people and things in the children's immediate surroundings. In this unit, the focus is on the neighbourhood. It includes a range of drawing techniques – pictorial maps, X-ray drawing, section, elevation, plan, observational drawing, blind drawing and designs. Pupils will have the opportunity to work with drawing in these different ways to increase their awareness of their physical and social environment; to help them reflect on familiar surroundings; and to encourage personal and emotional responses to the built and natural environment, and to people and things. It will help

develop their observational, analytical and interpretative skills, while extending their visual and verbal vocabulary, and introducing a range of drawing techniques.

AIMS

This unit offers children the opportunity to:

- collect and share ideas, and explore and experiment with materials
- develop the confidence to use a range of drawing strategies and techniques
- understand that marks can have meanings
- develop control over a variety of drawing tools and materials, using them selectively and purposefully
- look at different kinds of drawing, talk about them and try to interpret them.

ASSESSMENT FOR LEARNING

Assessment should focus not only on how well pupils can draw, but also on what each child learns through drawing – the knowledge, skills and attitudes that are developed through the use of drawing. How well a child can draw will be indicated by the confidence with which they engage in drawing activities, their skill in using tools and materials, and discrimination in using appropriate drawing strategies. Cues for how well drawing is aiding the learning process will be in how the act of drawing prompts children to reflect on experience, to question, wonder and generate ideas. By the end of this unit, pupils should be able to reflect on and rework their experience through drawing, and explore and share ideas.

▶ **CD-ROM RESOURCES**
- Presentation: Drawing outside
- Artworks and images
- Resource sheets:
  - What do you think?
  - Drawing ideas
- Teacher assessment
- Pupil self-evaluation

SESSION I **BUILDINGS: X-RAY VISION**

LEARNING OBJECTIVES
Children will:
- learn to use drawing to support their imagination by representing space in different ways
- learn to use drawing to develop spatial concepts by considering the relationships between inside and outside
- use drawing to record and illustrate relationships.

VOCABULARY interior, exterior, plan, elevation, section, X-ray, ground floor, first floor, storey

▼ RESOURCES

- ▸ doll's house
- ▸ A3 paper
- ▸ felt-tip pens
- ▸ CD-ROM: selection of pictorial maps

▼ ASSESSMENT FOR LEARNING

Can the children:
- ▸ draw an effective representation of the structure of seen or imagined buildings?
- ▸ begin to use drawing conventions, such as plan and side views?
- ▸ use drawing as a vehicle to discuss and represent ideas about homes?

ACTIVITY

Begin the session with a discussion about different ways of drawing buildings. Ask pupils to look through their drawings to find examples of analytical drawings, narrative drawings, annotated sketches and bird's-eye views of buildings. Encourage the children to identify drawings done from observation, memory and imagination, and those based on photographs. They may be the work of individual pupils or the result of a group effort. What are the advantages and disadvantages of different types of drawing? If necessary, introduce ideas such as, *Drawing can describe and explain things and it can help us to imagine what we cannot see from direct observation.*

- If possible, borrow a doll's house for the children to explore, and relate its external appearance to the internal space. This exploration could be done over a period of time, whereby pupils focus on different rooms and record their ideas in their sketchbooks.
- As a class or in groups, talk about and then draw on the whiteboard the elevations of the doll's house as accurately as possible. (If appropriate, some work on measurement and scale may be introduced.) Then, open up the house and ask pupils to draw the arrangement of the rooms, both as a section and as a plan.
- Now ask the children what their own home looks like on the outside, from the front, side and back, and challenge them to draw the elevations. (If it is a terraced house, then probably only two elevations, front and back, are possible.)
- Next, invite pupils to imagine what they would see if the walls were made of glass, or if they could open up the house, just like a doll's house. Ask them to choose one of the elevations as a basis for an X-ray drawing, to show the rooms that lie behind the façade and what they look like. They should include furniture and fittings to illustrate the different uses of the rooms. Keep these drawings for later discussion.
- Use the drawings and discussions of children's own homes to begin a discussion about homes from another time or place. What were homes like in the past or in other places, and why? For a Victorian terraced house, you might ask:

- *Who lived there? What kinds of people? How many?*
- *What building materials were used? Which construction methods?*
- *How were the houses lit and heated?*
- *What services did they have, such as running water and waste disposal?*
- Challenge pupils to draw a plan, an elevation and an X-ray drawing of a house from another time or place and to annotate them.
- Display the two sets of drawings showing their own home and a house from another time or place, side by side. Ask pairs of children to consider how homes have changed and why. Challenge them to list ten things that have changed and ten things that have remained the same. In this way pupils can begin to consider differences in the origins of products that retain a superficial resemblance and explore

social and economic differences. Pupils can present their findings in a plenary, referring to their drawings if needed.

DIFFERENTIATION

Children who have not progressed as far...
Pupils who are less confident can continue to explore the doll's house and practise drawing the inside and outside.

Children who have progressed further...
Pupils who have worked confidently and enthusiastically can make a 3D version of the X-ray drawing. Using a box to represent the building, they can prepare X-ray drawings of the four elevations and paste them onto the box.

SESSION 2 **PLACE: PICTORIAL MAPS**

LEARNING OBJECTIVES
Children will:

- develop the confidence to draw what they know, see and remember
- develop skills to represent places using pictures and symbols, and begin to understand plan perspective
- discuss and reflect on drawing and work together, engaging in shared decision-making
- learn to represent space by investigating different kinds of map.

VOCABULARY distance, direction, position, public building, public space, heritage, route, road junction, natural form

RESOURCES

▸ paper
▸ fibre-tip and felt-tip pens, marker pens
▸ colour washes
▸ photographic images of the neighbourhood
▸ examples of old pictorial maps and contemporary tourist maps
▸ CD-ROM: images of houses, building plans and elevations
▸ resource sheets: Drawing ideas

ASSESSMENT FOR LEARNING

Can the children:
▸ draw willingly and confidently without inhibition?
▸ construct simple but effective symbols?
▸ discuss their collaborative working and identify improvements in decision-making?
▸ explain what their drawings represent?

ACTIVITY

This activity involves pupils working from both memory and observation. It is in two parts and could take place over a number of lessons – the first is based on individual mental maps; in the second part, the children work together on a large-scale pictorial map of the school's catchment area.

■ Give each child paper and felt-tip pens and explain that they are going to draw mental maps of what they can remember of their neighbourhood. Encourage them to think about the different types of building in the area – domestic, commercial and public – such as houses, shops and the community centre. Are there any significant buildings that are an important part of their heritage? They should include public spaces, such as parks and cemeteries, and private spaces, such as gardens. Elements of natural form and networks of roads and pathways should be identified where possible.

■ Ask pupils to draw their home in the middle of the paper and work outwards from there in all directions.

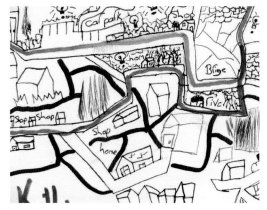

It does not matter which way up they use the paper. Some pupils might work best with a partner or teaching assistant to provide some support.

■ Allow enough time so all pupils can complete their drawings. The drawings should then be laid out on the floor and discussed together. The two key ideas that should inform the discussion are: content of ideas and method of representation. Drawings by children who live near each other can be compared to see if they have remembered similar things.

■ Discuss similarities and differences between plans and pictures – both are drawings. Show examples of old maps and tourist maps, which include illustrations as well as symbols. Follow with a discussion of plan perspective, where a drawing can be read from any direction – top, bottom, left or right.

■ Prepare a large outline map showing the position of the school at the centre and the key routes that radiate from it; indicate where certain neighbourhoods lie in relation to each other. Ask each child to work on a particular area of the map. It is probably more convenient to organise this in sections that fit together, so children can work in small groups at tables or on the floor, working from any direction. The finished sections can then be pieced together and the completed map displayed on the wall.

■ Encourage pupils to refer to their individual mental maps and to the examples of maps that you have introduced for ideas about ways of representing buildings, open spaces, natural forms, roads and any special features. Children should work with fibre-tip pens, making clear line drawings at first, illustrating what is to be found in the neighbourhood. They can invent symbols for trees, public buildings, sport grounds, car parks and so on.

■ Further discussion will be required among the children to decide how colour might be used – to identify the materials used on buildings perhaps, to differentiate between main roads and quieter roads, to identify fields and parkland, and water features, such as streams or ponds. Finally, colour can be added using felt-tip pens and colour washes.

■ Encourage pupils to undertake further drawing tasks, such as those in the **Drawing ideas** resource sheets.

DIFFERENTIATION

Children who have not progressed as far...
Pupils who are less confident can continue to work on their individual mental maps to elaborate them further by adding more information.

Children who have progressed further...
Pupils who have worked confidently and enthusiastically can prepare a key for the group map.

SESSION 3 NATURE: CLOSE ENCOUNTERS

LEARNING OBJECTIVES

Children will:

- learn to record images and ideas from memory and first-hand experience using a sketchbook
- learn to experiment and investigate by using different tools and surfaces to show tone
- learn more about artists' work from other cultures and time periods.

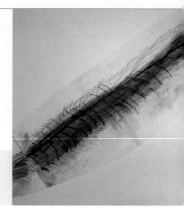

VOCABULARY shape, form, surface quality, pattern, texture, tone, weight, speed, pressure

▼ RESOURCES

- selection of simple and more complicated natural forms, such as plants (living and dried), bones, twigs, stones, shells, feathers
- A3 paper
- 2B, 4B and 6B pencils
- pencil sharpener
- resource sheets: Drawing ideas

▼ ASSESSMENT FOR LEARNING

Can the children:

- use a sketchbook with confidence to capture ideas and images?
- experiment freely using a range of drawing media, trying out and combining different types of mark?
- talk briefly about an artist they have studied?

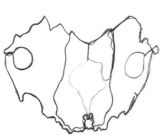

ACTIVITY

Make a display of natural objects, selecting a range of items made of different materials for the children to explore qualities of shape, form, tone and texture.

■ Invite some pupils to choose an object and discuss it with a partner. Then ask them to tell the class what they find interesting about it, what it feels like to the touch and what it reminds them of. Help them by elaborating and introducing new vocabulary. A stone might be shaped like an egg and have a smooth, cool feel to it. A piece of moss may be damp and velvety to the touch. You could make two lists – one of adjectives and one to suggest connections with sensory experiences.

■ Before drawing the objects, do some experiments with the pencils. B is a soft pencil; 6B is six times softer and can give a range of dark, grainy marks. Suggest that the children explore what different kinds of mark can be made with these pencils – drawing with the

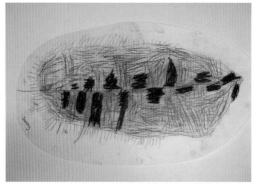

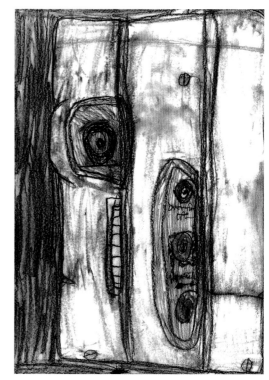

tips and sides; drawing fast and slow; and drawing strong and delicate lines. Can they create a smooth, strong, dark line, as well as a lively, delicate line? Can they draw with heavy and with light pressure, and at different speeds, to create a range of tones?

■ Ask them to create a range of three tones – light, medium and dark. Then ask if they can invent two extra tones somewhere in between. Pupils should use both sharpened and blunt pencils in their investigations.

■ A quick display of the children's efforts will prompt them to share how they created different sorts of marks. This can be used as a mini-plenary

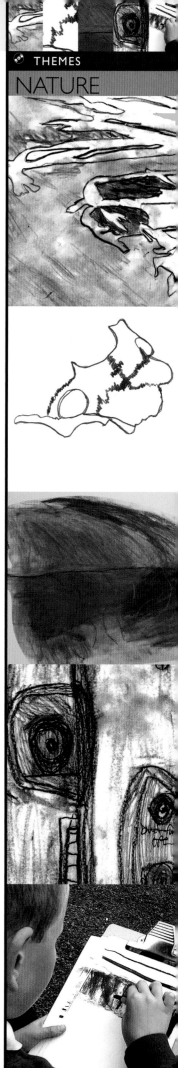

session and will provide an opportunity to assess children's understanding.

■ Explain that you will ask pupils to make a pencil drawing of an object. This will be from observation, and they will be expected to study it very closely, and analyse all the parts of its structure and surface. The drawing will not be a picture of the thing – it will be more of a record of how the child has struggled to understand the object. It will not be possible to use an eraser, as there will be no mistakes. If a mark is 'wrong', pupils should keep making marks until they are satisfied that they have created the 'right' one.

■ Rather than draw an outline shape and fill it in, ask pupils to draw from the inside of the form to the outside edge, responding to changes in line, shape and surface quality. Instead of looking at the whole object, advise them to concentrate on small parts of it. Urge them to look at the object rather than at their drawing.

■ When pupils have completed their drawings, put them up for everyone to see. Ask each child to choose a drawing (not their own) and say

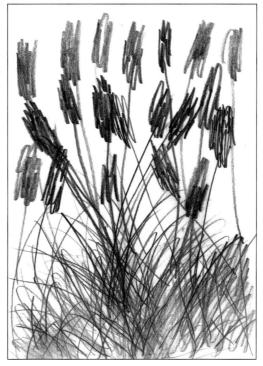

something positive about it – the qualities the person drawing has noticed, or the different ways in which the pencil has been used.

■ As an extension, groups of children could research objects used by artists in a variety of time periods and cultures. Their observations could then be presented to the class for discussion.

■ Encourage pupils to undertake further drawing tasks, such as those in the **Drawing ideas** resource sheets.

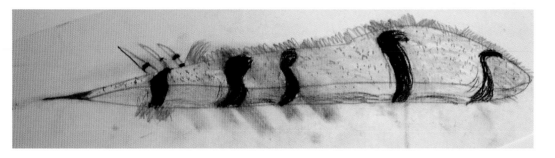

DIFFERENTIATION

Children who have not progressed as far…
Pupils who are less confident can be given closer guidance and more practice in how to observe and draw at the same time. They could be shown examples of drawings by others – perhaps simple drawings by children's book illustrators – to provide further examples of techniques they might use.

Children who have progressed further…
Pupils who have worked confidently and enthusiastically can do another observational drawing, but this time they should use the hand they do not normally write or draw with. They could be shown examples of more complex work by different artists and challenged to develop their work along similar lines.

SESSION 4 **PEOPLE: PAST, PRESENT, FUTURE**

LEARNING OBJECTIVES
Children will:
- gain confidence in their ability to collect and develop ideas using a sketchbook
- learn to improve their own work by discussing the drawing of others and considering how it might influence their own work
- recognise that artists often use drawing as a starting point for work they might carry out in other media.

VOCABULARY portrait, past, present, future, appearance, personality, character, occupation

▼ RESOURCES

▸ old photographs of people (some examples on the CD-ROM)
▸ range of drawing media
▸ CD-ROM: Artists' drawings of people
▸ resource sheets: Drawing ideas; What do you think?

▼ ASSESSMENT FOR LEARNING

Can the children:
▸ develop their creativity by using sketchbooks freely and purposefully to invent and record ideas simply?
▸ talk about the work of others, showing an ability to make simple judgements about the effectiveness of these works?
▸ understand that drawing can be used to gather and present different ideas for future work?

ACTIVITY

This activity is in three parts – drawing from photographs of people; drawing portraits of family from observation; and drawing a self-portrait from imagination.

■ Invite pupils to bring in old photographs of family members. These should be photocopied and labelled, and the originals returned to their owners at the end of the school day. (Alternatively, you could supply photocopies of other family photographs.) Lead a short discussion about who the photographs represent, what work the people might have done and what kind of people they might

have been. What are the clues – the clothes they wore, the setting in which they were photographed, their stance, appearance, and the expressions on their faces?

■ Give each child a photocopy of an image of a person and ask them to make a drawing to interpret what they see. They will probably have to guess at the colour of the clothes (as the photocopies will be in black and white), and may omit or add elements to emphasise certain ideas about their chosen person. Follow this with a discussion, asking the class to compare the photographs and the drawings,

commenting on what has been observed and what guesses have been made about people and their lives.

■ Show pupils the CD-ROM images. Ask them to reflect on and discuss drawings by artists such as Van Gogh, Stanley Spencer and Josef Herman, showing workers in the fields, the shipyards and the mines, and to make comparisons with the work people do today. If time permits, show at least one example of a drawn cartoon and the finished painting, and discuss the role that drawing plays in painting.

■ Challenge the children to draw portraits of family members when they go home, using materials of their choice. The drawings should emphasise facial characteristics, the way the person's hair is done, their expression, and the way they stand or sit. Ask them to find out about the various jobs that members of their family do.

■ In the following lesson, lead a discussion about these drawings, making mention of all the different jobs, professions and industries the children's families work in. Create a small gallery of the drawings, putting each drawing in a frame. The occupation or industry could be concealed for other classes to determine from the drawing alone. Clues could be provided in the form of symbols on attached labels.

■ Ask pupils what work they would like to do when they leave school. How do they see themselves in 20 years' time? Invite them to look at the list of jobs identified so far and decide if they wish to do one of these, or something different. Challenge them to draw how they see themselves in the future – oil pastels would be a good choice of medium to use. Put the drawings on display and let everyone have a go at guessing what job the person wants to do.

■ Revisit the photographs, the artists' drawings and the drawings pupils have done. Ask the children to decide what makes a good portrait, either in a photograph or a drawing. Pupils can use the resource sheet **What do you think?** to review their drawings.

DIFFERENTIATION

Children who have not progressed as far...
Pupils who are less confident should be encouraged to practise drawing from photographs and from direct observation. Their repertoire can be enriched by looking at the work of a range of artists and illustrators.

Children who have progressed further...
Pupils who have worked confidently and enthusiastically can make two further self-portraits. One that shows them now, as reflected in a mirror; and another made from a photocopy of this, modified to show them as a character from the past. They can be further challenged to discover new techniques for drawing from books in the school library.

SESSION 5 **THINGS: AWARD**

LEARNING OBJECTIVES

Children will:

■ learn to observe, analyse, investigate, invent and communicate ideas and information by drawing purposefully

■ learn to extend their skills and repertoire of drawing by experimenting with an increasing range of drawing media and tools

■ understand that drawing for different purposes will lead to different stylistic conventions.

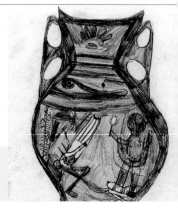

VOCABULARY **trophy, celebrate, award, achievement, value**

▼ RESOURCES

▶ pencils
▶ coloured pencils
▶ scraperboards
▶ CD-ROM: images of awards, cups and trophies; images of Greek vases

▼ ASSESSMENT FOR LEARNING

Can the children:

▶ create drawings with the clear intention of communicating ideas?
▶ use tools with confidence to develop an increasing range of texture, tones and shapes?
▶ adapt their drawing styles for different purposes?

ACTIVITY

Prior to the session, ask pupils to find out about trophies that they, the school or their parents have won. What form do they take – a silver cup, a shield, a crystal bowl or something else? Start the session by asking them to report on their findings. Discussion should focus on what the prize or award was for and how this was symbolised.

■ Talk to the children about awards. Cups, trophies and awards are given to athletes, stars of stage and screen, authors, artists – and even teachers – to acknowledge their work and achievements. This is a long-established tradition. In Ancient Greece, the 'vases' that were presented to athletes were more likely to contain precious oils than flowers. The scenes that decorated the vases celebrated athletic prowess together with cultural activities, such as singing and dancing.

■ Encourage pupils to make sketches of trophies at school or at home and, if possible, provide time for small groups to do this at the local secondary school or in your local town hall or sports club. These sketches will provide some reference for their later work.

■ Show the children images of Greek vases from the CD-ROM and allow them time to study them. Discuss ideas related to the Olympic Games, sports events, competitions and awards. The modern-day Olympics create opportunities to celebrate sporting prowess. Are there other areas of our lives that we should celebrate? Ask pupils what they would give an award for outside of the sporting scene. Ask, *What or who should we value in our lives? What achievements or special actions should*

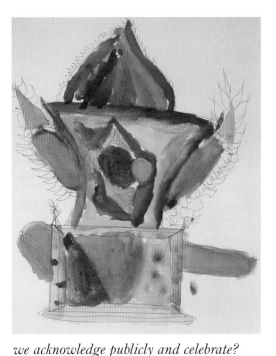

we acknowledge publicly and celebrate?

■ Invite small groups to discuss what is important in our lives – good deeds, looking after people, helping others, bravery – and encourage the children to think about people who deserve recognition.

■ Explain to the children that they are going to design a new award. Invite each group to decide what their award will be for and ask them to discuss possibilities as to how this should be symbolised. Ask, *Will it be for an individual or a group? The trophy is intended to be displayed and admired. Ask, Will it take the form of a cup, like the FA Cup, or a vase or a bowl? Will it be a sculpture – like the Oscar? What will it be made of – ceramic, bronze or glass, or something else? How will it be decorated? Will there be any words on it?*

■ The design activity should involve a series of drawings. The children can start by making annotated sketches to identify awards and prizes that have been discussed. They can then

consider the nature of their new award and what it aims to recognise, and draw scenes or illustrate phrases connected with it, such as 'helping hands', 'brave fire-fighters', or 'loving mother'.

■ Ask each group to select the best idea from these to prepare a final design for their award: either a traditional 'cup' or 'vase' form on which an illustration is incised, or a new sculptural form on which a symbol is incised, or which might even represent the shape of the symbol. The design can be done on scraperboard and include the scene or symbol to be incorporated in the award.

■ Finally, gather the children in a plenary and ask them what parts they enjoyed when carrying out the activity, and any part they may have found difficult. Can they say why?"

DIFFERENTIATION

Children who have not progressed as far…
Pupils who are less confident can revisit the idea of an award and draw a scene from the award ceremony.

Children who have progressed further…
Pupils who have worked confidently and enthusiastically can develop their skills in the use of scraperboard.

OTHER AREAS OF LEARNING

GEOGRAPHY

- The children's maps of the neighbourhood can be compared with Ordnance Survey maps. Pupils can use OS symbols to make a map of an imaginary neighbourhood.
- Pupils can make a traffic count on the way to school by tabulating the different vehicles they see. Then, on a length of till roll or long piece of paper about 7cm wide, they can draw all the cars, vans, lorries, buses and bicycles they have observed. Paste the rolls onto a large sheet of paper to create a 'traffic jam', then discuss their journey to school.

LITERACY

- Pupils can make a study of traffic signs and find out what they represent. They can then explore the use of symbols that stand for complex ideas, such as peace, love, happiness, friendship, war, danger and speed.
- Children can invent a family of paper dolls to illustrate the people who live in the doll's house. They can also make paper clothes to fit them and make up stories about the characters and their life in the house.

PHYSICAL, SOCIAL AND HEALTH EDUCATION (PSHE)

- Pupils can work in groups to design an illustrated leaflet that shows games that can be played in the playground to promote health and fitness.
- Children can develop techniques for critique – how to say something positive about someone else's drawing; how to find something of interest in it; how to make a suggestion for what might be improved.

Drawing

ICT

- Observational drawings of natural forms can be scanned into the computer. Pupils can use a simple drawing programme to modify and transform them to create new forms.

MOVEMENT

- Pupils can make shadow drawings of plants, or leaves on trees moving in the breeze. They can try to capture the changing positions of the shadows on paper on the ground.

MATHEMATICS

- Simple plans can be made to construct a doll's house.
- Pupils can use a grid to scale up drawings.

SCIENCE

- Diagrams can show systems for energy, water and waste disposal in a house.
- Pupils can use drawing to explore how things change over time in the life cycles of plants and animals.

HISTORY

- Pupils can draw different characters from history to show how people's clothes have changed over the centuries.
- Children can find out about how technology has changed the way we live in our homes. Using annotated sketches, they can show differences between a home now and a hundred years ago.

Painting is one of the principal areas of art and design practice and it can provide pupils with a powerful means of expression. They revel in the enjoyment of colour and will benefit from repeated opportunities to develop familiarity with its particular qualities. Ensuring that the focus is on the enjoyment and experience of paint, rather than on the production of 'finished' paintings, will help build confidence and dispel the feelings of frustration that can sometimes beset children at this stage.

Prior to Year 4, pupils will have had regular chances to develop painting skills, explore various starting points, and work on different scales with different media. Children's early experiences of colour-mixing in Years 1 and 2 will have been built on in Year 3, as will their initial discoveries about the potential of different kinds of paint and how it can be applied. In the painting unit of *Art Express* Book 3, pupils made simplified still-life paintings with a focus on pattern. They learned how to use viewfinders, compared compositions with one another and shared ideas.

In this unit, pupils explore the genre of landscape. They look at a wide range of examples and make comparisons between them, identifying common features and coming to a consensus about 'what is a landscape'.

The unit provides further options for pupils to work in sketchbooks, revisiting colour mixing, exploring the qualities of paint and making connections with the works of art they have explored. Pupils will share ideas about artists' approaches and use of materials, experiment with different techniques and, by the end of the unit, create two landscape paintings, one individually in watercolour and the other on a larger scale in collaboration with a partner.

AIMS

This unit offers children the opportunity to:
■ freely explore ideas, working from first-hand experience, memory and imagination and using a broad range of resources as a stimulus
■ experiment, on different scales, with different approaches to using and applying paint, with a wider range of media and painting tools
■ review, adapt and refine their own work, sharing ideas with others
■ begin to show a wider understanding of the works and ideas of different artists and increased confidence in describing colour, style and composition in paintings, expressing opinions using specialist vocabulary.

ASSESSMENT FOR LEARNING

This unit provides many opportunities to assess children's progress. The sessions aim to build pupils' skills and confidence, as well as their ability to respond to their own and others' work critically and constructively. Look out for pupils who, drawing on their own experience, start to make informed choices of materials and tools, and have the confidence to make decisions about the form their paintings will take, without adult intervention. Look also for evidence of children's developing understanding of artists' varied approaches and the ways in which they assimilate these into their own work, as well as their ability to articulate their understanding with a widening vocabulary.

▶ **CD-ROM RESOURCES**

■ Presentation: Making a landscape painting
   Masterclass
■ Artworks and images
■ Resource sheets:
   ■ Asking questions about landscapes
   ■ What do you think about this?
   ■ Thinking about landscapes
■ Teacher assessment
■ Pupil self-evaluation

SESSION 1 **WHAT IS A LANDSCAPE?**

LEARNING OBJECTIVES
Children will:

- learn about the features and genre of landscape painting

- learn to express their own ideas and opinions by describing and commenting on the work of different landscape artists.

VOCABULARY landscape, scenery, natural, rural, urban, townscape, seascape, representational, realistic, imaginary, Impressionist, abstract, idealised

▼ RESOURCES

- ▸ sketchbooks (one per child) or A4 paper
- ▸ pencils or pens
- ▸ a selection of landscape postcards or images from books, calendars and so on
- ▸ poster-sized reproductions of landscapes to share with the whole class
- ▸ CD-ROM: images of landscapes
- ▸ resource sheets: Asking questions about landscapes; What do you think about this?

ACTIVITY

This session focuses on introducing pupils to the genre of landscape painting. You will need to gather together a wide-ranging assortment of images so the children develop an understanding of the different kinds of landscape that exist, including rural, urban, marine, desert and tropical. The session does not involve pupils in any actual painting but is important in developing understanding and setting the scene for the sessions that follow.

- Start by providing pupils with a collection of landscape postcards (or small pictures from books or calendars) to share in table groups. Provide time for simply looking and talking and then ask the children to classify the cards in different ways.

Watch to see what kinds of group they come up with. Anticipate that they may discover several categories, including country, town, beach, seascape, brightly coloured (or dull) paintings, landscapes with (and without) people or animals, in spring, summer, autumn or winter. Challenge the children to make further sub-categories, such as seascapes with ships, rural landscapes with mountains and so on.

- Next, give each pair of pupils a small collection of cards or pictures (three or four) to look at in more detail. Ask them if they can come up with a definition of the term *landscape*. Then get the pairs talking to one another, and see whether they can arrive at a consensus definition. Some common definitions are: a painting of natural scenery; an expanse of scenery that can be seen in a single view; or a painting (or representation) of a real or imaginary scene.

■ Now show the whole class a broad range of landscapes using the images from the CD-ROM. Your selection should comprise different kinds of rural, urban, marine, desert or tropical landscapes so key features, similarities and differences can be identified and described. Include, if possible, interpretations of the same subject matter by different artists (such as Derain, Monet and Homer's different versions of the Houses of Parliament), as well as different scenes painted by the same artist. Invite pupils to point out common characteristics, and talk about different viewpoints and perspectives. Encourage them to use vocabulary such as *background, foreground* and *middle ground*. If you are using an interactive whiteboard, the interactive drawing tools can be used to highlight different characteristics.

■ Select one image to focus on in more detail. Ask pupils some questions about it – you can use the **Asking questions about landscapes** resource sheet as a prompt. Talk to the children about what they *know* from looking at it (what they can actually see in the picture) and what they *think* (what they can deduce or infer from what they see). Model examples of this distinction, such as: *I know there are trees on the hillside. I think it must be autumn because the branches are almost bare.*

■ Finally, give pairs of children a landscape postcard. Place it in the centre of a page of one of their

sketchbooks or on a sheet of A4 paper, or use the **What do you think about this?** resource sheet. On one side, ask them to consider and write four or five 'What do you know?' statements and on the other side a similar number for 'What do you think?' The writing part is less important than the discussion that the questions generate. Pupils could also use individual whiteboards to record their ideas.

▼ ASSESSMENT FOR LEARNING

Can the children:
▸ recognise and describe common features of landscape paintings, talk about similarities and differences they observe and show a developing knowledge about the way in which artists work?
▸ comment on work by different artists using subject-specific vocabulary to articulate their thoughts?

DIFFERENTIATION

Children who have not progressed as far...
For the oral activities in the session, these pupils may benefit from sensitive grouping with children who will allow them a voice in small-group discussions. Equally, they may be supported by being partnered with another child who could scribe their thoughts during the paired part of the activity.

Children who have progressed further...
These pupils should be expected to carry out more comprehensive research and express their responses to the genre with more sophisticated vocabulary. They might collect and organise research in a variety of ways and could be given extra time to do this.

SESSION 2 **COLOUR AND MARK**

LEARNING OBJECTIVES
Children will:
- reaffirm their knowledge of colour-mixing and mark-making by exploring mark-making and different consistencies of paint, with reference to several works of art by landscape painters
- learn to describe and comment on their progress.

VOCABULARY **deep, bright, dull, paler, darker, lighter, stronger, brighter, natural, runny, thick, watery, swirling, directional, sticky, daubed, dribbled, stippled, transparent, opaque, textured, scraped, scratched, splattered,** *scraffito,* *impasto*

▼ RESOURCES

- ▶ a selection of landscape postcards or images from books, calendars and so on by artists such as Cézanne, Constable, Vlaminck, Bierstadt, Van Gogh, Braque, Thomas Moran and Derain
- ▶ viewfinders
- ▶ acrylic or ready-mixed paint in the following colours: two blues (cobalt or Prussian blue, and ultramarine or brilliant blue), two reds (vermilion and crimson), two yellows (brilliant yellow and lemon yellow) and white
- ▶ palettes, mixing plates, water containers
- ▶ a range of brushes
- ▶ sketchbooks (one per child)
- ▶ an assortment of small cut (or torn) pieces of paper with different surfaces, for example, sugar paper, heavyweight cartridge paper, tracing paper, smooth shiny paper
- ▶ PVA glue
- ▶ palette knives, sticks of card, lolly sticks, plastic clay tools, scrapers
- ▶ small pieces of card
- ▶ glue sticks

ACTIVITY

In this session, pupils will try to match the colour and texture of paint they have seen in landscape paintings.

- Provide a range of landscape pictures for the children to look at. Suggest that they talk in their groups (and perhaps jot down ideas on individual whiteboards) about what different colours they can see and how the paint has been applied in each work. Elicit from them as many words as they can think of to describe what they are seeing and list these words on the class whiteboard as they contribute them. Help to extend the list by adding words that pupils may not be familiar with, such as *daub,* *stipple* and *scraffito.*
- Explain to the children that they are going to see whether they can match the colours and marks they can see in a sample of the paintings. Give them viewfinders to help them to select a

small area to focus on. Remind them of some of the basic 'rules' about painting that they will have practised in previous painting units, such as keeping colours clean by regularly washing their brushes; starting with lighter shades and gradually adding touches of darker colours; and using brushes in different ways.

- Suggest that they each make four or five of these small experimental pieces – swapping with others on their table and trying to match as closely as possible the colours and brushstrokes that the artist has made. One or two could be painted directly onto the pages of the children's sketchbooks; the remainder onto the prepared sheets of cut or torn paper. Some pupils may be very painstaking and produce fewer but very accurately reproduced pieces, while others may

work more quickly and make several. Lay these out and flatten them once dry – they will be assembled later onto a double sketchbook page.

■ Introduce pupils to the term *impasto* to describe paint that is applied very thickly. Add a little PVA glue to some acrylic or ready-mixed paint and let the children experiment with wooden or card sticks, palette knives or plastic clay tools (or anything that can be used as a scraper) on small pieces of card to get a feeling for applying paint in this way. Model how to spread the paint thickly, scratch into it (*scraffito*) and make swirling, directional marks with different tools.

■ Once these are dry, spread out all of the pieces and talk to the children about the challenges they encountered in making them. What were the difficulties, if any? What differences did they notice when using shiny paper

or more absorbent sugar papers? Were some colours harder to match than others? Did the colours alter as they dried? Encourage all of the children to articulate something about the process. Then ask them to arrange their own pieces to fill a page of their sketchbook and stick them down using glue sticks. Alternatively, a 'working wall' could be created, focusing on landscape painting, and the work created in this lesson used as the starting point.

▼ ASSESSMENT FOR LEARNING

Can the children:
▶ match colours they see in works of art, mixing from a limited palette of primary colours to recreate textural qualities with an assortment of brushes and tools?
▶ describe the differences in colours and textures they have created, using appropriate vocabulary?

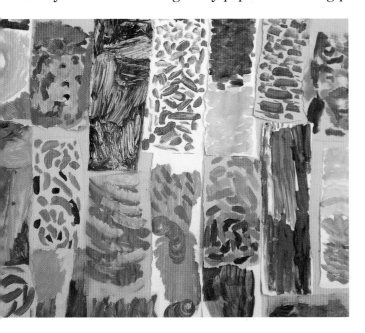

DIFFERENTIATION

Children who have not progressed as far...
These pupils may need help deciding what to add when trying to match specific colours. They may need a demonstration of some of the marks they could make – holding a brush or palette knife in different ways, for example – to extend their repertoire.

Children who have progressed further...
These pupils should be able to match subtle colour differences more easily and may describe their findings with a more developed vocabulary. They could be challenged to make a more extensive range of colour combinations. They may persevere longer at the task, needing additional time.

SESSION 3 **DEVELOPING IDEAS FOR LANDSCAPES**

LEARNING OBJECTIVES
Children will:
- learn to explore ideas and compositions by working from a combination of their own ideas and selected visual resources
- learn to talk about their ideas and give reasons for the choices they make.

VOCABULARY foreground, background, middle ground, horizon

▼ **RESOURCES**

- selection of landscape images for each table, including posters (see Session 1)
- sugar paper strips, folded to make four squares
- pencils
- fine line, medium and thick black pens
- viewfinders
- sketchbooks
- Presentation: Making a landscape painting Masterclass
- resource sheets: Asking questions about landscapes; Thinking about landscapes

ACTIVITY
This activity presupposes that pupils have looked at a lot of different landscape paintings and have had an opportunity to talk about what they contain. The session could be started by briefly revisiting the images used in session 1, including those on the CD-ROM, or by showing the class a series of landscape paintings in reproduction form."
- Remind the children of the different kinds of landscape they talked about in Session 1 (and the definitions they arrived at) and reiterate the many ways in which the features of a landscape can be arranged. Talk more generally about how landscapes can be real or imaginary and suggest to them that artists can sometimes create an edited version of nature by combining a number of elements from different places in their work. Focus on two or three images and, using positional vocabulary, ask the children to describe where things are in the paintings and where else they could alternatively be sited. The **Asking questions about landscapes** resource sheet can be used as a guide.
- Explain to the children that they are going to draw four landscapes and that each one will be different. Distribute a few landscape reproductions on each table. They should not copy the images but they can use the artists' landscapes for inspiration and to suggest the content of their own version – palm trees, a river or a path, mountains or a clump of cypresses, for example. Model for them a couple of times the process of looking at several pictures and taking from them elements that you then reassemble to make a new arrangement. Draw these fairly rapidly so the children see that this is not a painstaking and detailed drawing activity but a way of playing with different ideas, and therefore quick sketching is required.
- Encourage the children to look at several examples and to include a lot of different features in their four small

landscapes. They can use a viewfinder if they find it helps them to focus. Once they have drafted their four landscapes they can go back to each one and work on it using finer or thicker pens to add more detail.

■ When these sets of drawings are completed, spread them out and gather the children around to look at and talk about what they have done. Tell them that they are going to choose one of their set of four that they will scale up and develop into a watercolour painting during the next session. Encourage them to talk within their table groups about their choices or pair them so they can decide with a partner.

■ As an additional activity or for those who finish this more quickly, the children could be introduced to the **Thinking about landscapes** resource sheet, which focuses on landscapes in

different seasons. It asks the children to consider, with a partner, how the same scene would look at different times of the year. Alternatively, this could be given as a homework task.

▼ ASSESSMENT FOR LEARNING

Can the children:
▶ select from reference material and develop ideas to adapt and develop for their own use?
▶ generate several different compositions from which to choose an idea to work on in more depth?

DIFFERENTIATION

Children who have not progressed as far...
These pupils may struggle with the notion of not copying but taking from other works of art ideas to use in their own. They could work with a partner, sharing ideas about different landscape features to include, or be supported by a teaching assistant. Some may find a viewfinder helpful in isolating aspects of a picture.

Children who have progressed further...
These pupils may respond readily to the notion of selecting different elements of a landscape from reproductions of artists' work and combining these in their own drawings. They could be challenged to find out something about the history of landscape through internet research.

SESSION 4 WORKING WITH WATERCOLOURS

LEARNING OBJECTIVES
Children will:

■ gain the confidence to experiment with different approaches by using and applying paint freely to express their ideas for a landscape

■ develop their capacity for self-assessment by talking about their own work and that of their peers, and adapting their work in the light of these discussions.

VOCABULARY opaque, translucent, intense, thick, thin, watery, light, dark

▼ RESOURCES

▸ landscape sketches made in Session 3
▸ squares of watercolour paper (or good-quality heavyweight cartridge paper)
▸ pencils
▸ watercolour tins
▸ sketchbooks
▸ good-quality fine nylon brushes
▸ sponge brushes
▸ water containers

ACTIVITY

In this session, pupils will revisit the use of watercolour paints and do a short practice activity in their sketchbooks. Then they will make a small watercolour painting chosen from one of the landscapes they drafted in Session 3.

■ Distribute squares of watercolour paper and ask the children to draw out lightly the design they chose in Session 3 using a sharp pencil. Tell them not to worry about fine detail, but just to draft in the main shapes. They should use the pencils very lightly as, given the translucent nature of watercolour paints, any heavy lines may otherwise remain visible in the final painting. Now set these preliminary designs to one side.

■ Before starting the paintings, pupils will need to be reminded of how to use watercolour paints. Show them how to make a thin wash or a deeper, more intense colour by brushing the surface of the colour tablet lightly or more persistently until the strength of the pigment increases. Challenge the children to apply a single colour across a double page of their sketchbook, layering the paint in delicate washes and gradually in more intense versions, using both sponges and fine brushes. They can make whatever marks they like on their page – stripes, random patches, organised lines of pattern and so on. The purpose here is solely to re-familiarise themselves with using watercolour and represents a warm-up activity before they make their actual painting.

■ Redistribute the watercolour paper so pupils can start on their paintings. Suggest that they lay down the

background colours first, and then gradually build up layers of colour before adding pattern and decoration. Remind the children that they should choose larger brushes for the initial washes of colour and smaller ones to paint fine detail.

Part way through the session, stop and bring pupils together to review what they have done so far. Draw their attention to different responses – to different ways in which shapes and colours are being combined, or ways in which paintings are being worked into and detail added. Ask the children to pause and think about their own piece of work (and any changes or improvements they might make to it now), or suggest that they ask a partner (a 'critical friend') for advice about their work.

■ When the paintings are finished, pose questions for the children to answer with their partner, encouraging them to talk about what they enjoyed most and any part of the activity they may

have found difficult. Ask them to comment on their own piece of work and to think about anything they might do differently another time. You might also ask want to ask them to identify another child's work that they especially like and encourage them to justify their choice.

▼ ASSESSMENT FOR
   LEARNING

Can the children:
▶ show willingness to experiment and demonstrate an increasing understanding of paint and painting techniques?
▶ use a developing vocabulary to talk about their work, responding positively to advice and making refinements to their work in light of such advice?

DIFFERENTIATION

Children who have not progressed as far...
These pupils may need reminding of the kinds of mark they can make with brushes and watercolours in the initial practice activity. Help them by providing words for them to respond to (for example, *wavy, spiky, curly, dotty, loopy*) and encouraging them to fill the page with marks.

Children who have progressed further...
These pupils may show confident use of their sketchbooks to experiment with watercolours and make an extensive range of marks and shades of colour. They should be encouraged to take their explorations further – for example, to look at the different effects of using watercolour on wet paper.

SESSION 5 WILD (AND WONDERFUL) LANDSCAPES

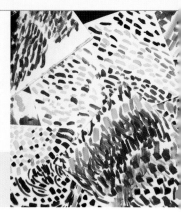

LEARNING OBJECTIVES
Children will:
- consolidate their practical skills by exploring mark-making in the manner of the Fauve artists, using a variety of tools
- learn about the landscape paintings made by the Fauve artists with a particular focus on the way colour is used.

VOCABULARY **See Sessions 1 and 2**

▼ RESOURCES

- ▷ examples of Fauve paintings, such as postcards, posters, calendars (some examples on the CD-ROM)
- ▷ acrylic paint, ready-mixed paint or tempera blocks in the following colours: two blues (cobalt or Prussian blue, and ultramarine or brilliant blue), two reds (vermilion and crimson), two yellows (brilliant yellow and lemon yellow), and white
- ▷ palettes and water containers
- ▷ a variety of large and small brushes
- ▷ sketchbooks
- ▷ large sheets, A2 or larger, of white card or heavyweight cartridge paper (one per pair)
- ▷ pupil self-evaluation sheet

ACTIVITY

In this final session, pupils will look at a selection of landscape paintings by artists such as Derain, Vlaminck and Braque (known as the Fauve artists), try to recreate some of the colours and marks they observe, and then work in pairs to create their own shared idea of a Fauve landscape. Since there are two distinct parts, this activity could be broken down into shorter sessions.

- On the whiteboard, show the children a selection of landscape paintings by the Fauve artists (see the CD-ROM). Ask them to describe what they can see in the paintings and talk to them about the broad, short strokes of bright contrasting colours that the paintings have in common. Ask the children to say what they think of the paintings. Explain that these were a radical departure from traditional

landscape paintings in the early years of the 20th century when they were created. They were consequently considered to be quite outrageous and were much maligned by the art critics of the time.

- Distribute some examples of Fauve paintings for the children to see close up and ask them to try to emulate, in their sketchbooks, the strong, directional brush strokes and vibrant colours they can see. If they are using paints they have not used for a while, you will need to remind the children how to use them. For example, pupils using tempera blocks may need to be shown how to work the surface of the

block with their brush in order to achieve a rich consistency of paint and strong colour.

■ Then ask pairs of children to plan a painting between them, drawing on ideas from the Fauves and from the selection of images they used in Session 3 when drafting their watercolour paintings. These will be much larger paintings and pupils will need to negotiate with one another what will go where and who will be responsible for painting the different parts of it. Suggest that they make a couple of quick sketches in one of their sketchbooks and then lightly draft their chosen idea onto the A2 card provided for each pair.

■ During the time that the children are working together, stop them every now and again to draw to their attention an aspect of somebody's painting for discussion.

When the paintings are complete, finish the session by reviewing what the children have done (and over the remainder of the unit) and what they have learned about landscapes. Elicit their views orally or ask them to complete the **Pupil self-evaluation** sheet. Display all the paintings alongside the children's sketchbook work and landscape drawings, together with some of the source materials that inspired them.

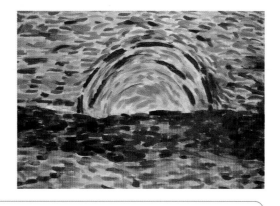

▼ ASSESSMENT FOR LEARNING

Can the children:
▶ agree ideas and work cooperatively with a partner in the process of planning and executing a joint painting?
▶ describe, compare and express opinions about selected landscape images using relevant vocabulary?

DIFFERENTIATION

Children who have not progressed as far…
Careful pairings may be necessary to ensure pupils work with a partner who supports but does not dominate the process. These children will benefit from being shown again how to create different Fauve-type marks with their brushes, while using the relevant vocabulary.

Children who have progressed further…
These pupils are likely to make more connections between the marks they make in their paintings and those of the artists' work, and try to achieve more varied effects. They could be encouraged to find out more about the Fauve artists as a homework task or a research task in class.

OTHER AREAS OF LEARNING

ICT

■ Explore the work of landscape artists on the internet using a website such as the Web Museum (www.ibiblio.org) as a starting point. Pupils could choose an artist and focus on their range of work or look at landscapes over a particular period or featuring a particular place.

■ Make a *PowerPoint* presentation to inform others about landscape paintings.

HISTORY

■ Children could find out more about the history of landscape painting by researching from books and the internet, guided by you, or as a homework task. Their research could be used to make a leaflet, booklet or *PowerPoint* presentation (see ICT).

■ See what pupils can find out about past times by looking at landscapes – paintings (by artists such as Avercamp and Bruegel) reveal a wealth of information about the time and place where they were made and especially how people lived in the past.

■ Explore the seasons through a range of landscape paintings.

DRAMA

■ Create a drama based around characters within a landscape, lost in a landscape or wanting to develop or preserve a landscape.

MATHEMATICS

■ Encourage the use of mathematical language, especially vocabulary relating to fractions and position, to describe the whereabouts of elements within a landscape painting and the space they occupy.

■ Encourage pupils to notice the horizontal, vertical and diagonal lines that divide up landscape paintings.

Painting

ART AND DESIGN

■ Link this unit with a local environment study or rural school trip. Sketching and taking photographs of 'real' landscape views is the best source to use back at school.

■ Investigate the colour green. Mix paints, inks and dyes in primary colours to create dozens of shades. Use them to paint sheets of paper and store these for collage activities.

■ Use these collage papers, plus glossy pictures from holiday brochures, to create imaginary exotic landscapes – 'my holiday heaven'.

LITERACY

■ From a collection of a dozen or more landscape postcards, let groups of pupils decide and justify which six should be chosen for an exhibition. Children will need to use persuasive arguments to ensure that their favourite makes the final cut.

■ Describe a landscape painting that children can't see and ask them to draw what they visualise from your description. This activity encourages sustained concentration and close listening. It also requires good oral skills on the part of the person describing the details.

PHYSICAL, SOCIAL AND HEALTH EDUCATION (PSHE)

■ Allocate pupils different roles within groups, to make scripted presentations about what they have learned about landscape. To build self-esteem, ensure that each child feels included.

■ Create opportunities for pupils to have a 'critical friend', to work collaboratively – sharing ideas, problem-solving, and to discuss how well they worked together.

By Year 4, pupils should have built an understanding of several different printing methods. They should be able to talk about prints they have made and discuss ideas for using the methods they have learned in different ways to produce a variety of results. The children should also recognise that printing is hugely important in our culture and society, and that we rely on it daily for communication, work and leisure, as well as using it as an art form in its own right.

Prior to Year 4, children will have been given opportunities to use a range of printing materials and techniques, to develop their motor-control skills, build planning and prediction skills, and use relevant vocabulary. Alternative ways of applying colour will have been introduced, encouraging pupils to make choices and create their own designs from stimuli. The definition of printing will have been reinforced so they understand that it usually involves pressing together either a hard surface and a softer one to produce an impression, or two surfaces with colour applied to one.

In this unit, pupils are introduced to further materials and media that can be used for making prints (such as string and plastic clay) and are offered opportunities to extend the application of previously introduced media (such as cloth and polyprint) to begin to recognise their versatility and potential. The sessions are supported by carefully selected images on the CD-ROM to inspire the children and bring out the best in each method, and a Presentation showing a specific printing technique.

As well as providing clear instruction, each session is carefully structured to build on the previous one, and to utilise and extend the skills gained in the printing units in *Art*

Express Books 1, 2 and 3. Pupils should feel encouraged to find creative ways of solving printing problems and meeting printing challenges.

AIMS

This unit offers children the opportunity to:
■ learn to make prints in a variety of ways, building on previous experience, and experiment creatively with a range of methods
■ develop practical skills through techniques requiring a greater degree of motor control and different materials and equipment
■ discuss and recognise the potential of different techniques, and predict and modify results
■ make connections between their work and that of other artists, times and cultures, and use a variety of artworks as inspiration for their prints.

ASSESSMENT FOR LEARNING

Assessment is ongoing throughout the unit, with specific questions accompanying each session – for example: *Can pupils talk about the similarities between their prints and the artworks they have studied?*

The sessions also include challenges and problem-solving activities to produce evidence of specific skills and thought processes, such as: *Challenge the children to suggest ways in which lines could be printed.*

Further questions for assessment are also suggested at the end of each session, and on the resource sheets.

> **CD-ROM RESOURCES**
> ■ Presentation: Modelling clay prints Masterclass
> ■ Artworks and images
> ■ Resource sheets:
>   ■ Cloth printing
>   ■ String printing
>   ■ Plastic clay printing
> ■ Teacher assessment
> ■ Pupil self-evaluation

SESSION I CLOTH PRINTS FROM AN OBJECT

LEARNING OBJECTIVES
Children will:
- learn to experiment creatively by making prints in an alternative way
- extend their understanding of how printing inks behave by considering methods of application and drying times
- learn to discuss, plan and modify the printing method to achieve the best possible results
- learn about the practice of a contemporary working artist.

VOCABULARY pounce, apply, polycotton, cloth (avoid using the word *material* as this is ambiguous), **three-dimensional, drape, dispense, recall, avoid**

▼ RESOURCES

- ▶ small toy cars
- ▶ clay, paint and paper for initial experiments (optional)
- ▶ thin white polycotton cloth
- ▶ fabric scissors
- ▶ old socks and stuffing (to make pounces, see Session 5 in the printing unit of *Art Express* Book 3)
- ▶ printing inks
- ▶ printing trays
- ▶ printing rollers
- ▶ bucket or sink of water
- ▶ other three-dimensional textured objects (baskets, broken alarm clock, old mobile handsets, dried corn cobs, toys)
- ▶ CD-ROM: images of Stacey Chapman's car
- ▶ resource sheet: Cloth printing

ACTIVITY

Show the class a toy car. Invite pupils to suggest ways in which it could be used to create a print. They may suggest pressing its roof into clay, or running its tyres through paint and then over paper. Try these, and any other suggestions, if you wish, either at this stage with individual volunteers or later as part of the practical session.

- Show the CD-ROM image of the print of Stacey Chapman's car and ask how this might have been made. The car was inked all over and a cloth pressed onto every part of it. Show the second image, where this is being done. Invite the children to try producing a similar print using a toy car. Challenge them to recall the best way to apply ink to an uneven object. (This is an opportunity to revisit and reinforce the work done with the pounce in *Art Express* Book 3 – for

details, see below.) Ask pupils to work out the order in which things should be done. For example, the pounce should be made, and the cloth cut to fit the car first, as the ink will begin to dry as soon as it is rolled out.

- Pupils should first cut their cloth large enough to drape over the entire toy car. Invite them to say why the piece should be cut from the edge of the cloth and not the middle! Next, they should make a pounce by stuffing the toe of a sock with a soft rag. (See Session 5 in the printing unit of *Art Express* Book 3 for the full method.)
- Ask the children to describe how to prepare an inking station, then challenge them, in groups of two or three, to set up their own by pouring 2cm of ink at the top of their printing tray and rolling a thin, sticky skin of ink over the tray's surface with the roller. (This technique is introduced in Session 3 of the printing unit in *Art Express* Book 2; see also the step-by-step instructions in the Presentation: **Ink/roller technique** Masterclass of the accompanying CD-ROM. This technique is reinforced throughout the printing unit in *Art Express* Book 3.)
- Ask pupils to recall and describe how to pick up ink with the pounce and apply it to the toy car. The pounce should be lightly pressed and rolled on the inked tray, then applied to the car's surface using the same movement.

■ When the car is fully inked, discuss how to lay the cloth on it, the aim being to get the best contact between all the surface areas. The cloth should be pressed carefully all over the car, avoiding slipping, and then peeled off.

■ Discuss the results. If they are not satisfactory, make further attempts and also experiment with inking and printing from other objects.

■ Stacey Chapman used a fire hose to clean her car! Don't forget to wash ink off objects before it dries or put them in the bucket or sink of water straight after peeling off the cloth, to be washed later.

■ The **Cloth printing** resource sheet can be used to consolidate the work covered in this session.

▼ ASSESSMENT FOR
   LEARNING

Can the children:

▸ competently carry out the method of cloth printing and suggest and talk about other objects they can use?

▸ explain why they have used certain tools and why tasks have to be done in a particular order?

▸ talk about their decisions when carrying out the work and say how they reached them?

▸ describe the project carried out by Stacey Chapman and make links between it and their own work?

DIFFERENTIATION

Children who have not progressed as far…
These pupils may have difficulty controlling the pounce or applying the cloth accurately. Set simpler challenges, such as applying the ink to flat surfaces with the pounce and smoothing the cloth over them.

Children who have progressed further…
These pupils may be given more complex challenges, such as larger objects that have to be tackled with a larger team, or applying more than one colour. They can also be asked to draw the car both three-dimensionally and flattened, as if for a folding template to make a model car.

SESSION 2 **STRING PRINTS**

LEARNING OBJECTIVES
Children will:

- gain confidence in experimenting creatively with line by making prints inspired by linear artworks
- develop further practical skills by manipulating equipment and materials in a controlled and specific way

- extend their understanding of the versatility of the method
- gain confidence in using the work of other artists to inform their own thinking.

VOCABULARY linear, register, inspiration, manipulate

▼ RESOURCES

- pencils and drawing paper
- very stiff card (greyboard) cut into squares approximately 10cm x 10cm
- Copydex glue
- small, flat containers, such as jar lids
- plastic glue spatulas
- string of different thicknesses
- scissors
- printing inks, rollers and trays
- newspaper
- paper (for printing designs on)
- CD-ROM: images of Artists' linear artworks

ACTIVITY

Show the images from the CD-ROM and ask what they have in common. All the artworks include linear design – shapes, patterns or images formed from lines. Challenge pupils to suggest ways in which lines could be printed.

- Demonstrate to the class how to make a string block. To do this, start by drawing one or two very simple lines on one of the card squares. Dispense a very small amount of Copydex glue (it dries quickly – add more only as you need it) into a lid.

(PVA can be used, but the block must be allowed to dry for 24 hours before inking. With Copydex, the block can be used immediately.) Next dip the spatula into the glue *vertically* and use it vertically to tap a thin raised line of glue along the drawn lines. Find the end of the ball of string and feed it gradually along the glue line, pressing it gently into place. Cut the string only where necessary – the ends can be trimmed more neatly once the glue is fully dry.

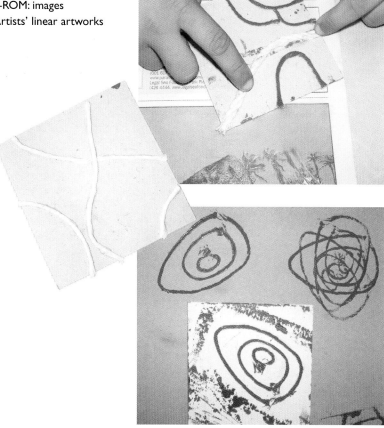

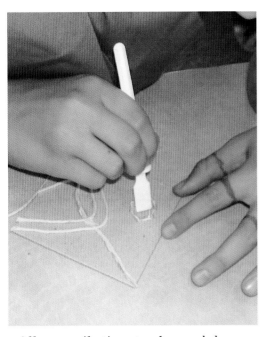

■ Allow pupils time to plan and draw their design on paper, using the CD-ROM images as inspiration. Urge them to use simple lines so that the string can be manipulated easily along the design. Ask the children what should be done if one line crosses another. Can they work out that the string must be cut so that it does not pass over another piece of string? Can they understand that only the highest point would make contact with the paper when the block is used for printing?

■ When the children are happy with their designs, ask them to draw them onto their pieces of card. They can then apply the string as demonstrated.

■ While the blocks are drying, pupils should set up their printing stations with an inked tray, clean and inky rollers and newspaper pieces. The children should trim any protruding string from the edges of the block and place the block on the newspaper.

■ The children can now ink up their block with the inky roller, register it on the paper and roll it with the clean roller to take a print.

■ Pupils can experiment with the resulting prints by using more than one block, turning the block in different directions, overlapping prints, using different colours or adding thicker string to the block and making a further print over the original. Which versions do they like best?

▼ ASSESSMENT FOR LEARNING

Can the children:
▶ suggest and/or experiment with variations on the technique to achieve different results?
▶ control the string and the glue and follow the instructions accurately?
▶ talk about similarities between their print and the paintings they have studied?
▶ show evidence of the influence of the artworks they have studied in their own design?

DIFFERENTIATION

Children who have not progressed as far...
These pupils may need encouragement with their design and help with making their string block. Focus on the process of inking up the block and registering it neatly, reinforcing the sequence. Avoid trying different ideas until the children have mastered this.

Children who have progressed further...
You can set further challenges for these pupils from those listed in the last bullet point above, including collaborating as a team to produce a joint print.

SESSION 3 **TUBE STRING PRINTS**

LEARNING OBJECTIVES

Children will:

- understand how to experiment creatively with the block to achieve varied results
- learn to create a continuously repeating print by making a cylindrical block
- learn to recognise and make links between continuous designs on fabrics and papers and their own work.

VOCABULARY As for Session 2, plus **repeat pattern**, **continuous**, **cylindrical**

▼ RESOURCES

- ▸ examples of linear repeat patterns, such as on fabric, wrapping paper or wallpaper (some examples on the CD-ROM)
- ▸ cardboard tubes cut to fit inside printing trays
- ▸ pencils
- ▸ Copydex glue
- ▸ small, flat containers, such as jar lids
- ▸ plastic glue spatulas
- ▸ string
- ▸ scissors
- ▸ printing inks, rollers and trays
- ▸ newspaper
- ▸ paper to print on
- ▸ CD-ROM: images of Artists' linear artworks
- ▸ resource sheet: String printing

ACTIVITY

Revisit the work done in Session 2, looking at the artworks used for inspiration, the method for applying glue and string and the results of the string-block printing. Ask pupils how a repeat pattern has been achieved with this method (by re-inking and re-registering the block each time).

Display the images of the wallpaper, fabric and wrapping paper. These are linear repeat patterns, but they are continuous, with no visible joins. Challenge the children to suggest ways in which this effect could be achieved. It may help to ask what causes the visible joins between prints – they are there because the block has edges. Can the children work out that if a cylindrical rather than a flat block were to be used, the print could keep repeating?

■ Invite pupils to make a string block as in Session 2, but this time on the surface of a tube. They can either draw their design on the tube first, or simply stick the string on gradually. Ask pupils to recall why the string must be of one thickness and must not cross over other lengths of string.

■ While the glue sets, roll the trays with ink. The children can then roll their tube in their inked tray.

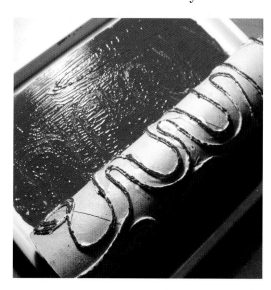

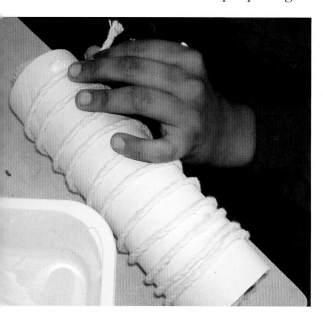

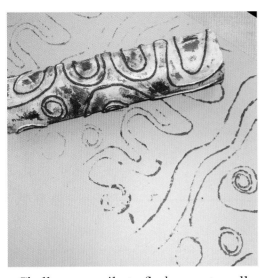

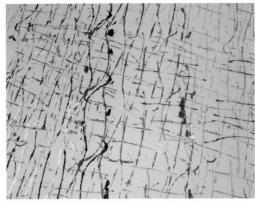

Can the children:
▸ show evidence of trying several ideas?
▸ design and make the cylindrical block and explain why the print it gives will differ from a flat block?
▸ share and discuss ideas with others and make clear plans for further experiments, explaining what they hope to achieve?
▸ talk about examples of where this method is used in the wider world?

■ Challenge pupils to find ways to roll the inked tube on the paper without getting too much ink on their hands. This can be done by inserting the fingers into each end of the tube and manipulating it from inside, inserting a wooden roller longer than the tube, or by putting the fingers in between the string patterns on the surface and 'walking' them round the tube.

■ A wide variety of results can be achieved. See Differentiation for further ideas. You can add thicker string between the original string on the tube and create an over-print in a contrasting colour. Draw the children's attention also to the intriguing prints formed by the tube in the inked tray.

■ Challenge pupils to think of other cylinders that repeat a print. These might include car tyres on a muddy track, a pastry cutter or a paint roller. There are also special rollers that can be bought at DIY shops to create print effects such as knotted wood.

■ Offer the children a design challenge to use the knowledge they have now acquired. This could be to design and print wallpaper for a dolls' house, wrapping paper for a particular festival or fabric for a specific costume. Alternatively, pupils could design and make a cylindrical block to print a border for a bathroom wall or a decorative edge for a piece of writing.

■ The **String printing** resource sheet can be used to revisit and consolidate the work covered in Sessions 2 and 3.

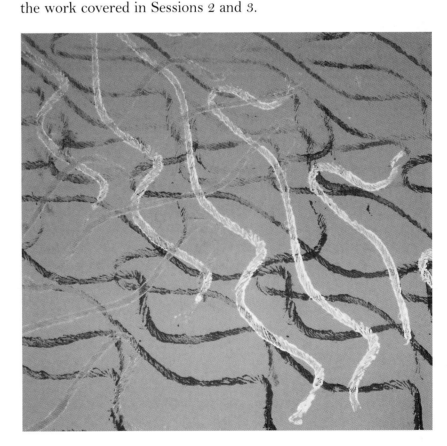

DIFFERENTIATION

Children who have not progressed as far...
These pupils may need help with applying glue and string. If motor control is a problem, avoid pencil design and go for a very simple but effective idea, such as winding the string around the tube.

Children who have progressed further...
Offer these pupils design challenges, such as using more than one colour, printing in different directions or putting both these ideas together.

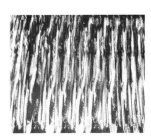

SESSION 4 **PLASTIC CLAY PRINTS**

LEARNING OBJECTIVES
Children will:
- learn to use natural forms and the work of other artists as inspiration for modelling and carving a block
- use the correct paint application method and pressure to create a clear print
- discover ways of changing the print and applications for its use
- learn about the connections between their own prints and those of other times and cultures.

VOCABULARY polyprint, transfer, surface texture, reference, alternating

▼ RESOURCES

- ▶ suitable stimuli (such as small leaves)
- ▶ walnut-sized balls of plastic modelling clay (you can use up pieces that are past their best, and it is useful to warm them first!)
- ▶ sharp pencils or spent ballpoint pens
- ▶ printing trays
- ▶ bottled paints
- ▶ dry bristle brushes
- ▶ damp, squeezed-out, flat sponges
- ▶ scrap paper
- ▶ paper to print on
- ▶ Presentation: Modelling clay prints Masterclass
- ▶ CD-ROM: images of woodcuts, etchings, and lino and block prints
- ▶ resource sheet: Plastic clay printing

ACTIVITY

Show the class the CD-ROM images of the woodcuts, etchings, and lino and block prints. What do pupils think they have in common? How do they think the prints have been produced? What kind of block would have been used to make them? Look at the images of the blocks. Can the children say how these blocks differ from the string blocks made in Sessions 2 and 3? Explain that the prints in the images were all created with carved blocks made of wood, lino or metal. The lines are carved into the block, rather than being applied to it and raised, like the string. Discuss how the carved blocks might have been made, the tools needed, how long it would have taken and the care that went into them. Would they be as easy to alter or correct as a string block? (Another carved-block technique, using polyprint with carved markings, is described in Session 5 of the printing unit of *Art Express* Book 2. An extension of this method will be used in the following session.)

■ Explain to pupils that they are going to try a method of making a carved block that, unlike wood or metal, can be altered or modified if necessary.

Set up stations for groups of two

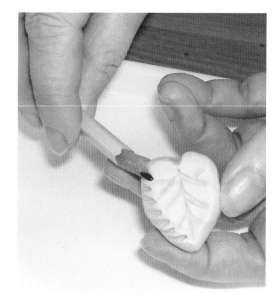

or three pupils and follow the instructions in the Presentation.

■ Prepare the block as shown, making sure that it engages fully with the surface of the tray.

■ Pupils should select a leaf and make careful drawings of it, observing the outer edge and the veins. Carve the block as shown in the Presentation (for help, see Differentiation).

■ Following the instructions, make your first prints.

■ The final two slides show only one possible idea. See Differentiation for further applications. When modifying the shape of the block (such as

lengthening or bending the tip of a leaf, or altering the veins), ensure that it is flattened against the tray and engages with every part of the surface before taking a print.

■ Invite the children to suggest useful applications for this technique. Examples include edging a piece of work or a greetings card, or creating a decorative border on a garment or along a painted wall. Challenge pupils to think of examples of a small, detailed print in the wider world. These might include postage stamps, coins, sealing wax on the backs of letters and date stamps on library books. Discuss the blocks that would

have to be designed to make each of these prints.

■ Use the **Plastic clay printing** resource sheet to consolidate the work covered in this session.

▼ ASSESSMENT FOR LEARNING

Can the children:
▸ show evidence of studying the leaf and the examples and using these to inspire their design?
▸ make a good attempt to follow the instructions and achieve a clear print?
▸ discuss and try out variations in colour, shape and design, and describe the results they hope to achieve?
▸ talk about the examples of prints shown and say how they relate to their own prints?

DIFFERENTIATION

Children who have not progressed as far...
These pupils may need help with carving, which should be neither a stroke nor a gouge, but a firm, clear line. Make sure that any loose bits of modelling clay are cleaned out of the grooves, and check these from time to time during printing. Do not allow blocks to get larger than walnut-sized – they are difficult to control and peel off, and can give poor results.

Children who have progressed further...
Challenge these pupils to try further ideas, such as modifying the shape of the block to print differently shaped leaves on one plant, varying the background paper colour, or suggesting other suitable small stimuli, such as shells or flowers.

SESSION 5 **EXTENDED POLYPRINTS**

LEARNING OBJECTIVES

Children will:

- learn to experiment creatively and purposefully with a further carved-block technique, building on previous experience
- develop practical skills by making and using smaller blocks and adding further carved detail

- make choices about their work, discussing shape, colour, texture and balance
- extend their understanding of how art and culture can influence their own work by studying architecture as inspiration.

VOCABULARY polyprint, transfer, surface texture, reference, alternating

▼ RESOURCES

- ▶ polyprint (thin polystyrene sheets)
- ▶ scissors
- ▶ printing inks, rollers and trays
- ▶ pencils or spent ballpoint pens
- ▶ newspaper
- ▶ scrap paper
- ▶ background paper
- ▶ CD-ROM: images of unusually shaped architecture
- ▶ pupil self-evaluation sheet

ACTIVITY

With the class, study the images of architecture supplied on the CD-ROM. Why do pupils think these buildings are considered unusual? What makes them different from the norm? Is it shape alone or are there other factors, such as texture, materials, colour and location? Why do the children think the architects

might have built them this way? Invite pupils to make drawings of the shapes they find most interesting. Explain that they are going to use one or more of these shapes as inspiration for their prints, and then add further layers of shape, pattern and colour over these prints to build up interest and texture.

■ Pupils should select a single shape from their sketches to transfer onto a piece of polyprint. For best results, the piece should be about 10cm square, as larger pieces can crack when peeled off the paper after printing. The shape can be transferred either by copying, cutting out the paper shape and drawing around it onto the polyprint, or laying it over the polyprint and pricking through the line with a pencil. Cut out the polyprint shape with scissors.

■ Set up a printing station for every two to three children. Discuss the colours of ink that should be used. Use the colours in the buildings to reach decisions, and remind the class that everyone can move to different stations to use different colours of ink. Mix the inks to the chosen colours and roll them thinly onto the trays.

■ Ask pupils to make choices about the surface texture of the block. They can leave it plain, and print a texture over it later in another colour, or mark into it with a ballpoint so the background paper colour shows through the print.

Encourage constant reference to the images of buildings. The photographs on these two pages all show prints inspired by Sydney Opera House.

■ Pupils should ink up the block in their chosen colour, remembering that other colours and shapes are to be added over the first layer of prints. It may be wise to choose pale colours as a first layer. Remember also that inks can be blended on the tray to achieve a bi-coloured print. Pupils should also take decisions about their background colour, perhaps using the building's location as inspiration.

■ Generate discussion about the next layer of printing, again referring to the buildings you are studying. Encourage the children to experiment with ideas – they can make further blocks, cut parts from their existing block, clean the block and change its colour, or mark the block with an old ballpoint or pencil. They should also consider its positioning on the paper – for example, overlapping or alternating with existing prints.

■ Continue printing until a balanced design is achieved. Ask volunteers to comment on how their own or a classmate's print reflects the building that inspired it.

■ At the end of the session, provide each child with the **Pupil self-evaluation** sheet for feedback on the work undertaken in this unit.

DIFFERENTIATION

Children who have not progressed as far...
These pupils may find it helpful to use fewer variations, such as two simple blocks with two contrasting colours, rather than cleaning, cutting and carving different blocks.

Children who have progressed further...
Challenge these pupils to work in a group to produce one joint large printed design, perhaps with larger blocks or using more than one building as a stimulus. This will stretch both their motor and their discussion skills and give you the opportunity to observe the ways in which they reach decisions.

OTHER AREAS OF LEARNING

LITERACY

- Invite pupils to write the diary of Stacey Chapman's car (Session 1).
- Linear artworks (Sessions 2 and 3) and unusual architecture (Session 5) could inspire descriptive poems.
- The Japanese woodcuts seen in Session 4 can be used as the basis for a *haiku*.

MATHEMATICS

- Use Sydney Opera House (Session 5) as the basis for work on sequencing and tessellation.
- Challenge pupils to work out the pattern sequences in the work of Bridget Riley (Sessions 2 and 3) and devise more colour and number sequences.
- Use the different grades of size in the sections of a pagoda (Session 5) to inspire work on fractions, area, proportion, size and ratio.

HISTORY

Use linear artworks as the basis of a history investigation.

- When were linear patterns first used on masks?
- How, when and why were Viking runes developed?
- Why and when did painters such as Picasso and Edvard Munch first began to experiment with line?

SCIENCE

- Compare plastic clay (Session 4) with other modelling materials, such as natural clay, air-drying clay and play dough, to see how each reacts to heat, cold and when used to make a printing block.
- Research how some of the manufactured materials used in the unit (plastic clay, polystyrene, polycotton) are made.

Printing

PHYSICAL, SOCIAL AND HEALTH EDUCATION (PSHE)

- Discuss how pieces of artwork can help a community of people? What is their purpose?
- How do pupils think we can solve the problems of boredom among young people and vandalism of public artworks?

RELIGIOUS EDUCATION

- Study the use of printing and pattern in sacred artwork, such as Islamic weaving and ceramics.
- Compare traditional church or cathedral architecture with the cathedral in Barcelona designed by Gaudí – what are the messages in this kind of building?

GEOGRAPHY

- Invite pupils to research where the raw materials used in the unit have come from – for example, cotton (cloth and string), tin (toys), wood (woodcuts) and stone (architecture). These can be marked on a world map.

MUSIC

- Use the work of Bridget Riley (Sessions 2 and 3) to inspire a sequenced composition, taking each coloured line in one of her paintings as a different note.

Collage or mixed media (the assemblage of materials and images to create new ones) and textiles (any kind of woven, knitted, hand-made, machine-made or non-woven fabric) both supplement each other in the classroom. Nature is a plentiful resource bank of images, motifs, shapes, patterns and colours. Responding to the world around us makes a wonderful starting point for cross-curricular work, as well as ensuring a richer and more meaningful educational experience.

Prior to Year 4, pupils will have explored collage and textiles through play and experimentation. They should have learned the way in which threads become fabric and how materials can be assembled to create new images. Dying, embellishing, joining, stitching, collating, painting, ripping and layering will all have been explored in some way. Building on these skills, the children will be expected to incorporate prior knowledge in their collaborative work with others.

In this unit, pupils are encouraged to respond to the natural world around them, incorporating observational drawing with detailed mixed-media work. Collaborative work is the focus, with an array of project ideas. Costume and ceremony is covered through the study of woodblock printed fabrics, and the children are encouraged to design their own motifs and patterns, as well as printing their own fabric. The sessions in this unit have the potential to take longer than individual lessons and the unit of work will form the basis for a sustained period of time.

AIMS

This unit offers children the opportunity to:

■ explore and comment on different starting points for collage and textiles work, using sketchbooks to collect visual stimuli, through drawings, photographs, notes and discussion, and, if possible, a visit to gain inspiration

■ investigate and explore different materials, changing the surface and appearance of paper by adding and layering other media, exploring patterns in fabrics, learning to make blocks and using them to make a range of marks and repeat images on fabric

■ develop and use an extended and broad vocabulary to describe collage and textiles, making comparisons and links to other techniques covered in previous years

■ compare and comment on the work of artists, photographers and craftspeople from around the world.

ASSESSMENT FOR LEARNING

During this unit, assessment should be ongoing, and should incorporate a wide range of recording methods, using photographs, samples, sketches and presentations, rather than just looking at the end results. Throughout this unit, pupils will widen their understanding of where materials, patterns and designs originate, and look to other cultures to make connections between fabrics, design and costume.

Group collaborations on collage work reinforce the way mixed media can incorporate observational drawing. Throughout, encourage reference to artists and craftspeople. Discussing ways in which pupils could make improvements to their own and others' work will help them to build confidence and communication skills.

► CD-ROM RESOURCES
■ Artworks and images
■ Resource sheets:
  ■ Rainforest factfile
  ■ Textiles quiz
  ■ Designing patterns
  ■ *Adinkra* stamps and symbols (1 and 2)
■ Teacher assessment
■ Pupil self-evaluation (1 and 2)

SESSION 1 INVESTIGATING RAINFORESTS UP CLOSE

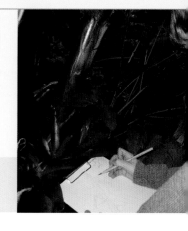

LEARNING OBJECTIVES

Children will:

- learn to explore and comment on different starting points by using cameras and sketchbooks to collect visual information
- learn to improve their work by discussing their ideas with others and making suggestions for improvements
- learn to present images from the natural world to show the fragility of the world's rainforests, their location and importance
- learn to compare and comment on the different approaches used by artists and photographers.

VOCABULARY **forest floor, forest canopy, understorey, emergent trees, orchids, epiphytes, aerial roots, drip tips, camouflage, climbers, deforestation, destruction, viewfinder, sketching, tone**

▼ RESOURCES

- ▶ viewfinders
- ▶ digital cameras
- ▶ sketchbooks (one per child)
- ▶ pencils
- ▶ black pens – fibre-tip, roller-ball or ballpoint
- ▶ CD-ROM: images of the rainforest

ACTIVITY

Ideally, this session should be held in a tropical house at a botanical garden or in a specialist indoor rainforest, such as the Eden Project, The Living Rainforest or At-Bristol. These offer valuable opportunities to sketch at first-hand the plants found in a rainforest, with the added benefit of being a convenient art, geography and science lesson. If this is not possible, make a display of tropical houseplants in the classroom, or show rainforest images on the interactive whiteboard (see the CD-ROM). Explain to the class that the aim of the session is to create a series of observational

drawings that focus on zooming in, in preparation for the creation of a large group collage.

■ Before the visit, have a preparatory discussion about rainforests, show the images from the CD-ROM and make links with any geography and science work. Use the vocabulary list above to explore new terminology.

■ Introduce the concepts of zooming in and close up. Discuss with the class different ways they could zoom in on their visit to the tropical house. In the classroom, you could use microscopes, digital cameras or visualisers to look in detail at hair, textiles, papers and leaves. (If available, use a visualiser or microscope that can project onto a whiteboard.) Talk about viewfinders and make some to take on your visit. (Cut out a small hole from black card in a shape that corresponds to the paper you are using, so sketchbooks would need a rectangular hole.)

■ During the visit, split pupils into groups (with helpers) to research different plants from the canopy, forest floor and understorey. Encourage photography, as well as sketching and recording the names (if possible) of the different plants in sketchbooks. The children can work in pencil, but black pen will allow you to photocopy the images back in the classroom.

■ Ask pupils to sketch the whole or major part of the plant, with at least

a couple of leaves. Then ask them to zoom in on one part and make an observational drawing of it (using viewfinders).

■ Talk to the children about sketching different plants, foliage and flowers, paying close attention to the shape of leaves, climbers and epiphytes. Encourage those who are progressing further to use viewfinders to find interesting compositions from a variety of plants. Remind pupils to annotate their drawings with

information that can be found on signs about the plants.

■ Each group will need to take a series of digital photographs as part of their visual reference. It is important to keep a log of which group has taken which photograph (rather than which individual child). Do this by asking each of the groups to choose a team name and write it on a sheet of paper, then photograph this before any of their reference shots.

■ Either during the visit or back in the classroom, gather the class together to discuss their sketches. If possible, lay the sketches out on the floor and talk about what has been recorded. Ask pupils to place their work according to the type of plants they have found, or group them into flowers, leaves, epiphytes and fruits. During this discussion, ensure that you reinforce the concepts of zooming in, close up, detail, design and composition.

▼ ASSESSMENT FOR LEARNING

Can the children:
▸ collect appropriate images and ideas in a sketchbook?
▸ use digital photographs and collected material as inspiration for their work in the classroom and show evidence of the starting point in their work?
▸ look at their work and that of others and talk about how they could make improvements or use their research in future work?
▸ talk about the work of an artist inspired by the natural world?

DIFFERENTIATION

Children who have not progressed as far...
Ensure these pupils are placed in groups with others who will be able to support them. Keep the tasks short and encourage them to feed back when finished. Give these children pens to discourage rubbing out and distraction. If necessary, use a timer to focus on drawing for one minute at a time.

Children who have progressed further...
These children may look very closely and spend more time adding fine detail to their work. Encourage them to work with their team, helping and leading where necessary. Give them a list of more complex vocabulary to research and use in their work. They could use a range of tonal pencils for sketching.

SESSION 2 **EXPLORING RAINFORESTS**

LEARNING OBJECTIVES
Children will:

- gain confidence in experimenting and develop further practical skills in the use of collage
- learn to reflect on their progress by examining their own sketches, notes and collage experiments in relation to others in the class

- learn about the work of a range of artists, illustrators and photographers who have created images of, or responses to, rainforests.

VOCABULARY collaborate, connect, detail, blocking, layering, overlap, enhance, perspective, distance, montage

▼ RESOURCES

- ▶ a good selection of artworks and photographs by contemporary artists and photographers who live or work in rainforests
- ▶ large sheets of sugar paper (one per group)
- ▶ glue sticks or PVA glue
- ▶ tropical houseplants, such as cheese plants and orchids
- ▶ sketchbooks
- ▶ pencils and drawing materials
- ▶ powder, block, acrylic or watercolour paints in two blues and two yellows
- ▶ brushes, mixing palettes and water pots
- ▶ oil pastels
- ▶ tissue paper
- ▶ *Where the Forest Meets the Sea* by Jeannie Baker (Walker Books)
- ▶ CD-ROM: images of the rainforest
- ▶ resource sheet: Rainforest factfile

ACTIVITY

Prior to the session, photocopy the children's sketches from Session 1 and print out the group photographs. The focus of this session is firstly to discuss the visit and undertake further research, and then to do some short practical activities in preparation for the group collage. This session could be spread out over a number of weeks as a series of short activities.

■ Soon after the visit, discuss the trip with the class, sharing findings and experiences. Ask, *What did it feel like? What did it smell like? What did you notice about the temperature?* Make links, where possible, with geography and science and look at the **Rainforest factfile** resource sheet.

■ Split pupils into groups with their photocopied drawings, photographs and sketchbooks. Invite them to create a montage of their findings on sugar paper. Then ask them to report back to the class in a mini-presentation.

■ Share with the children the work of a wide range of contemporary artists and photographers who live or work in rainforests (see also the rainforest images on the CD-ROM). Encourage pupils to research images on the internet and discuss issues of deforestation in groups or as a class. The children could also find out about the way in which people have caused the destruction of the rainforests and look at ways of trying to protect them.

■ Read *Where the Forest Meets the Sea* by Jeannie Baker, focusing on the relief collage images used to tell the story. Discuss what a collage is and what materials you could make it from. Ask, *What has been used in this book?*

■ The following four activities could be carried out on a 'carousel', with pupils moving on to different workstations around the room. Alternatively, plan to undertake the activities during different sessions.

■ Complement the sketchbook studies from the visit with drawings of tropical houseplants, such as cheese plants and orchids. This gives pupils the opportunity to handle the leaves (which is not safe or allowed in a tropical house) and discover more about the waxy structure.

■ Experiment with mixing shades of green. Use sketchbooks to reinforce secondary and tertiary colours (a colour wheel may be useful). See how many different greens the class can produce. (For greater variety, use two different yellows and blues, such as brilliant and lemon yellow, and cobalt and Prussian blue.) Use powder or blocks of paint (or watercolour or watered-down acrylic), rather than ready-mixed, for more subtle colour mixing. Paint on strips of paper and then stick into sketchbooks, or leave wet sketchbooks to dry before closing.

■ Use tissue paper to create a leaf, either on card or in sketchbooks.

Ask, *How can the tissue be used to create the stem or veins?*

■ Lay down blocks of tissue paper in sketchbooks in the shape of leaves or flowers, and then add acrylic paint, oil pastel or both over the top. Focus on adding features, details and highlights.

■ After experimenting with these ideas, discuss the outcomes with the class in preparation for planning a collage in Session 3. Discuss which paints were more effective. Ask, *How did you use tissue paper to create leaves? What happens when you add paint or oil pastel to tissue-paper collage? What happens if you add green paint to green tissue?*

▼ ASSESSMENT FOR LEARNING

Can the children:
▶ use a range of different starting points for exploring collage – for example, can they: mix more than ten greens; layer tissue and add paint or oil pastel on top; make comparisons between the different techniques; understand why this preparation work is important?
▶ work with others in a group to collate sketches and photographs, undertake research and ask questions about the rainforest?
▶ talk about the work of artists and photographers and the ways in which they represent the rainforest?

DIFFERENTIATION

Children who have not progressed as far...
Ensure groups are selected carefully, and encourage these pupils to make a contribution, using others to write down their ideas.
You could scan their drawings and allow them to create a *PowerPoint* display of their work.
Simplify the activities and focus on areas they need to improve on before continuing.

Children who have progressed further...
Encourage these children to combine techniques or find other ways to represent aspects of the rainforest. Encourage independent research of artists and rainforest images, as well as high-order thinking about the issues. This could lead to a class debate about the destruction of the rainforest.

SESSION 3 **GROUP RAINFOREST COLLAGES**

LEARNING OBJECTIVES

Children will:

- learn to experiment and investigate purposefully by using previously collected sketches, notes from first-hand experiences and direct observations to fuel their rainforest design
- gain confidence in evaluating their progress

- learn to change the surface and appearance of paper by adding other media
- learn more about a range of artists and photographers who have created images of rainforests.

VOCABULARY **collaborate, connect, detail, blocking, layering, overlap, enhance, perspective, distance**

▼ RESOURCES

- ▶ sketchbooks
- ▶ pencils
- ▶ watercolour paints
- ▶ brushes, mixing palettes and water pots
- ▶ sheets of thick sugar paper or cartridge paper (one A1 sheet and enough A3 sheets for each child, pair or group)
- ▶ tissue paper – as many greens as possible and a good range of natural colours (tissue is very effective, but you can also use colour swatches cut from glossy magazines)
- ▶ PVA medium (one per child) – stronger and less runny than standard PVA glue
- ▶ brushes or glue spreaders
- ▶ acrylic paint (use tubes as less gets wasted) and nylon fine brushes for fine detail
- ▶ oil pastels
- ▶ CD-ROM: images of Artists' rainforest paintings
- ▶ pupil self-evaluation sheets (1 and 2)

ACTIVITY

This session may be carried out over several lessons. Recap on Session 2, discussing the collage experiments and referring to the rainforest visit and the observation sketches created.

■ Explain to the class that initially they are going to design an imaginative rainforest in their sketchbook, building on the knowledge they have gathered and the experiments they have done in Session 2. Give them some boundaries – either to incorporate the whole rainforest, or just the canopy or forest floor. They might want to research animals, birds and insects if they want these to be included. Initiate a discussion of proportion and basic perspective to reinforce the sense of depth in the picture.

■ Give pupils watercolours and ask them to use these to plan their desired colours for the final group collage.

■ Next, encourage each group to contribute their ideas and draw them onto a single A1 sheet – the whole class drafting their designs together

on the one piece of paper. Pupils will need to communicate with others and to suggest areas that require further filling. Cut this plan into sections that relate to your class, group or pairs. Each child or pair should then enlarge the design from their section onto their own piece of A3 or sugar paper to create their part of the final class composition. You may want to take a photograph of the original group design to project onto the interactive whiteboard while each child works, to show the plan for the finished layout.

■ Bring the groups together to revisit the sketchbook work done in Session 2 and discuss aspects of using papers to lay down the initial colours. (You can use any papers, but in this example tissue paper has been used and then detail has been added in acrylic paint and oil pastel.) Talk about using a range of greens. Ask, *Where might light green be used, or dark green? What other colours can you see in the rainforest and where might they be used?*

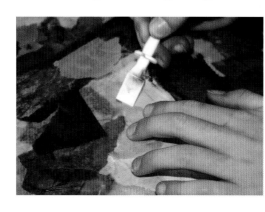

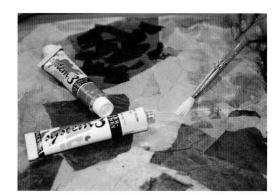

■ Encourage pupils to block out areas of colour with tissue paper and glue, either flat or raised to give features. Discuss aspects of composition and suggest that members of each group check that colours are consistent and match up when joined together.

■ Review the work in progress and the finished work by laying it out on the floor and standing back to see if any areas need to be worked on. When the collage aspect is finished, ask pupils to use oil pastels and acrylic paint to add detail or highlights. Tissue and glue will need to dry so you may choose to do this in a later session.

■ At the end of the session, ask all of the children to use the **Pupil self-evaluation** sheets to record their progress in this group project.

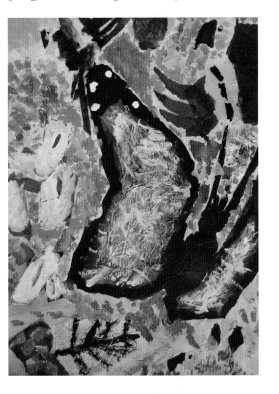

EXTENSION WORK

Photograph each collage and then transfer it to fabric using ink-jet transfer paper. Iron the results onto fabric to create a lasting rainforest image. This could be embellished with needlework, sequins or other media.

Alternatively, build on the skills acquired in the Collage & Textiles unit of *Art Express* Book 3 and use its Presentation to help create an artistic response to the rainforest using felt.

▼ **ASSESSMENT FOR LEARNING**

Can the children:
▸ incorporate their initial observation drawings in their final design?
▸ use a range of materials, selecting appropriate colours and textures for their purpose, and make use of skills from the previous session?
▸ work with others in the group to talk about how their work links together?
▸ talk about the work of artists and photographers and the ways in which they represent the rainforest?

DIFFERENTIATION

Children who have not progressed as far...
These children could work with a partner to create two adjoining sections of the collage. The task could be simplified by allowing them to use a photograph or poster as the inspiration for their section, rather than their imagination.

Children who have progressed further...
Encourage these children to add more detail to their work and really take care when cutting the tissue. Allow them to lead their team and make suggestions about improvements and joining of images. Suggest they show strong evidence of the development of their ideas in their work.

SESSION 4 **INVESTIGATING COSTUME AND TEXTILES**

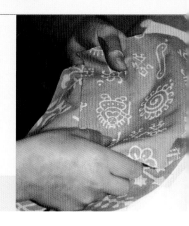

LEARNING OBJECTIVES
Children will:

- learn to experiment purposefully by investigating a wide range of fabrics, discovering their varying uses
- develop their practical skills and technical understanding by learning about early mark-making on fabric using natural pigments, in preparation for a later session on fabric printing
- start to understand the principles and techniques used in a range of different textiles and make comparisons between them using appropriate vocabulary
- learn more about the early skills of craftspeople from different cultures and prehistory.

VOCABULARY **daub, stamp, print, block, mark-making, cave art, prehistoric, cultures, tribal, tattoo, emblem, magical, mystical, spiritual**

▼ RESOURCES

- ▶ fabric swatch books, lots of different samples
- ▶ mud (from outside) and other earth pigments
- ▶ sketchbooks or paper
- ▶ sticks (for making brushes)
- ▶ a range of paint brushes (hog hair, sable, squirrel)
- ▶ cotton sheeting or calico, cut into A4 pieces and stuck to paper with masking tape (two per child)
- ▶ any available paint in earth colours, such as umber, ochre, sienna, reds
- ▶ fabric crayons in similar colours, if available
- ▶ natural items such as stones and feathers for making marks on paper or fabric
- ▶ CD-ROM: images of hand-painted items; textiles and clothing from around the world, including fashion items and wedding dresses
- ▶ resource sheet: Textiles quiz

ACTIVITY

In the first part of the session, pupils will find out about different fabrics and their uses in clothing or costume. In the second part, they will learn how early people decorated fabrics and began to make stamps, in preparation for their own block-making and printing activity in Session 5.

■ Split the class into four groups and give each group a section of the **Textiles quiz** resource sheet. Children can use a range of books and the internet to research the different types of fabric and record their findings in their sketchbooks. Bring the groups together to discuss the fabrics and

their uses. Ask, *Why are some fabrics more suitable than others for particular types of clothing? What would you make a wedding dress from? What might you use to create a ceremonial costume?*

■ Discuss with the class why people might want to decorate fabric. Cave painting led to decoration of human skin and then similar designs were applied to hide, skins or cloth with fingers, sticks and stones. Mud was the most accessible material for painting with and, by selecting it from different locations, the colour changed naturally. It could also be altered by adding other substances, producing

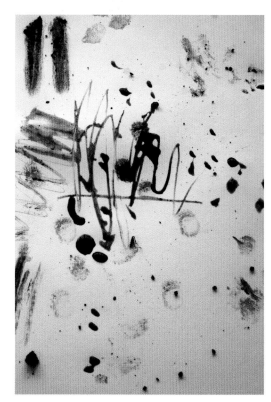

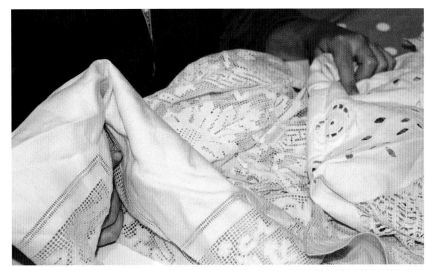

shades of black, red, yellow, brown and white. Ochre is a strong pigment used for its rich red colour to decorate hair, bodies and clothing. Umber, ochre and sienna are all important earth pigments still used in the painter's palette today.

■ If possible, go outside to look at soil colours. The children can experiment in sketchbooks or on paper using fingers, sticks and stones to make a range of marks with the mud. Ask, *What happens if you water mud down or add other pigments to it? What are the limitations of these materials for making marks? What might you want to do with your stick?*

■ Pigment was probably first applied to cloth by hand, and then with sticks. Later, sticks with frayed ends caused by chewing were used, and then brushes made by attaching animal hairs to sticks. Invite the class to experiment with making brushes from sticks. Investigate what brushes are made from (hog hair, squirrel, sable and so on). Use the CD-ROM images

to discuss different cultures and the importance of hand-painted motifs on cloth and decorative objects.

■ Using scraps of cotton sheeting, encourage the children to make marks with their own brushes and other natural brushes using paint in earth colours (browns, reds, ochre, umber) – supplement with fabric crayons if possible. You will not need fabric paint unless you want to wash the cloth.

■ Using objects or utensils to impress a repeat or similar design into pottery can be traced back to prehistoric times. Designs can also be stamped onto cloth using a range of natural objects such as shells, sticks or bones. Invite pupils to experiment with printing marks on fabric using items such as sticks, feathers, leaves, stones or shells.

■ In a plenary, discuss the differences between daubing and stamping paint onto fabric. Ask, *How do these differ? Why would you use one over the other? How would you create a repeat design on a piece of fabric? Which method would give quicker and more efficient results?*

▼ ASSESSMENT FOR LEARNING

Can the children:
▸ find out what different textiles are and what they are used for?
▸ make marks on fabric using a range of techniques used by early people, and recognise the difference between painting and stamping onto fabric?
▸ talk with others about their fabrics and present their ideas to the class through sketchbook, verbal or group presentations?
▸ find out about another culture that uses marks in a significant way to tell stories?

DIFFERENTIATION

Children who have not progressed as far...
Making marks should be accessible for all. If need be, limit the selection of materials and keep the tasks short and focused. Cut up the resource sheet and give these pupils a small selection of materials to investigate.

Children who have progressed further...
Encourage further study into prehistoric people and the ways in which they made marks and symbols. Expect these pupils to make more links between fabrics and uses. Encourage them to create a repeat design with the found objects and turn this into a story.

SESSION 5 **FABRIC BLOCK PRINTING**

LEARNING OBJECTIVES

Children will:

- learn to investigate by researching the use of printing in textiles and considering the use of motif in textile design
- develop further practical skills with reference to decoration of fabrics for ceremonial use
- learn to make comparisons between painted and printed textiles and use vocabulary to explain their work and motif designs
- learn about the differences between costumes worn in different cultures and their practical, ceremonial and decorative uses.

VOCABULARY **motif, repeat, ornamentation, geometric, naturalistic, stylised, abstract, line, dash, dot, mark-making**

▼ RESOURCES

- ▸ fabric samples – collected, images and/or educational fabric packs (from educational suppliers)
- ▸ Indian woodblocks (available from craft shops or educational suppliers)
- ▸ sketchbooks and pencils
- ▸ materials to make printing blocks – string, wood, potatoes or apples, press print, card and neoprene
- ▸ knife to cut potatoes or apples (adult only)
- ▸ glue spreaders
- ▸ printing ink (fabric ink if you intend to wash the fabric; you will need an iron to fix it) – use a thin, rolled out layer of printing ink or paint on a tray or palette
- ▸ cotton sheeting or calico – several small pieces per child for experiments; a large piece for a group print; individual pieces for scarves or costumes (laying the fabric on an old blanket or newspaper gives it a soft bed and helps the cloth absorb the ink better)
- ▸ resource sheets: Designing patterns; *Adinkra* stamps and symbols (1 and 2)

ACTIVITY

Prior to the session, ask pupils to collect fabric with motifs or designs, such as upholstery, cushions or curtain fabric, or borrow some swatch books from a fabric shop.

- Refer back to Session 4, and discuss the differences between stamping an object and painting motifs directly onto fabric. Discuss how a motif is created and where inspiration comes from. Look at examples of fabrics and use the **Designing patterns** resource sheet to explore ornamentation and sources of design. Children can use their sketchbooks to draw different examples from the fabrics studied.

If you have woodblocks, the children can try printing with these.

- Show the class a range of *adinkra* cloth images and woodblocks from Ghana in Africa, and talk about how *adinkra* is used in costume. The cloth is worn on a daily basis as well as for more special occasions. Dark *adinkra* cloth (black and red) is used for mourning dress. Brightly coloured cloth is called *kwasiada* (Sunday) *adinkra* and is used for celebrations and everyday wear.

- Study a range of *adinkra* symbols (see the ***Adinkra* stamps and symbols** resource sheets). The Ashanti of Ghana used

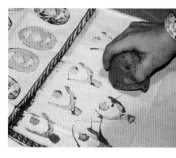

stamps cut from calabash shells (a type of gourd) to print their famous *adinkra* cloth. Each symbol has a different meaning – some spiritual, some magical, some allegorical. Discuss the meaning of these terms. Talk about which symbols represent man-made things and which natural things. Ask, *How would the cloth be printed?* The symbols are printed in groups on cloth marked into squares. The ink is made from bark boiled with iron slag. The stamps are dipped into this dark dye and pushed down onto the fabric. It dries to a black glossy finish.

■ Ask pupils to cut up the **Adinkra stamps and symbols** resource sheets and stick their favourite images into their sketchbooks. Then invite them to design a symbol of their own that has some importance to them (allegorical, spiritual or magical).

■ When the children have finished drawing their designs, ask them to talk to a partner about their symbol and its significance. Encourage each child to give a personal response and to resist copying their friend.

■ Explain to pupils that they are going to turn their design into a stamp or block, and they must choose one of the following methods: a potato (since the design is simple, this would work well but an adult will need to cut it); small blocks of wood decorated with string to create a line or built up with layers of cardboard; or neoprene foam glued with PVA adhesive. The neoprene foam is easy to cut with scissors. Press print could be used but would give a

reverse image from a block unless it was cut out rather than drawn into.

■ Challenge small groups of pupils to experiment with layering ink onto the block or stamp. Encourage them to work out which technique suits their block, remembering that each design will be printed a number of times.

■ Once the blocks have been created, lay out a large sheet of plain cotton sheeting or calico (or individual triangles for scarves). Divide the sheet into squares and ask each child in turn to print their design onto the cloth. You can paint the lines in between with brushes.

ASSESSMENT FOR LEARNING

Can the children:
▷ identify a motif in a piece of patterned textile and record evidence in a sketchbook?
▷ create a printing block that relates to their research and design?
▷ use appropriate vocabulary as part of their ongoing work and recognise how woodblocks or blocks produce work more quickly?
▷ talk about *adinkra* cloth and explain how it is used for formal and informal wear?

DIFFERENTIATION

Children who have not progressed as far…
Use a photocopier to reduce or enlarge these children's drawings to fit the block. They can then use tracing paper to help them transfer the design. Encourage them to take time to print their block, working with a partner who can offer assistance or modelling.

Children who have progressed further…
These pupils could experiment with creating a block in a number of different materials. They could design a piece of clothing that relates to *adinkra* and explore how to make it. Encourage them to print their design with precision.

OTHER AREAS OF LEARNING

SCIENCE

- Pupils can research the diversity of plant and animal species of the rainforest.
- Study the different layers of the rainforest – the forest floor, the understorey, the canopy and the emergents.

GEOGRAPHY

- Children can look at the different rainforests and locate them on a map of the world.
- Pupils can study the Amazon and the tropics.

Collage & Textiles

MATHEMATICS

- Pupils could undertake a project to work out the surface area of a variety of different-shaped leaves. The results could be tabulated and represented graphically – for example, in a bar chart showing numbers of leaves in a certain range of surface areas.

MUSIC, DRAMA AND DANCE

- Explore the movement of the animals and birds of the rainforest and compose music that reflects these creatures.
- Make a small dance or drama about a tale from the rainforest.

LITERACY

- Read *The Jungle Book* and other stories of survival and adventure in rainforests and look for imaginative narratives and descriptive language.
- Pupils can look for and read reports on the destruction of the rainforest, campaigns on behalf of the rainforest and debates on its destruction – the needs of people versus nature.
- Children can write about their own adventure in a jungle through a story, poem or song.
- Read a range of rainforest tales and stories, for example:

    Bloomin' Rainforests Anita Ganeri, Mike Phillips
    (Horrible Geography series, Scholastic)
    Up a Rainforest Tree Carole Telford, Rod Theodorou
    (Amazing Journeys, Heinemann Library)
    The Vanishing Rainforest Richard Platt, Rupert Van Wyk
    (Frances Lincoln)
    Journey into the Rainforest Tim Knight (Oxford University Press)
    Nature's Green Umbrella Gail Gibbons
    (Mulberry Books, William Morrow)
    Tropical Rain Forest by Donald M Silver
    (One Small Square, McGraw-Hill Professional)

Many artists and craftspeople around the world use recycled materials to make sculptures and artefacts. In many countries where raw materials are expensive and scarce, these materials have been used to make masks, due to their lightweight nature and strength. In this unit, children will learn about masks from different cultures and will make their own masks, using recyclable materials.

Prior to Year 4, children will have investigated the properties of recycled materials. They will have explored space and form and developed an understanding of the concept of three-dimensional structures by creating their own sculptures. They will have developed basic construction and modelling techniques using recycled materials and paper laminate to create a sculpture from direct experience. They will have begun to select materials for a particular purpose and developed their ideas, collaborating and co-operating within a group. As their work progressed, pupils will have discussed and made decisions about ways to improve their sculptures.

In this unit of work, children will build upon these experiences. They will use the Indian epic story the *Ramayana* as a stimulus, extending, developing and applying modelling and construction techniques to create a mask of a chosen character. They will develop their ideas from extensive visual research, by investigating facial expression from their own and each other's faces as well as the masks they have studied.

The children will plan how to make their masks, using their previous experience to help them to select and use materials to produce their ideas. Throughout the creative process, they will consider different ways to communicate their ideas, and there will be opportunities to evaluate and refine their work as it progresses.

AIMS
This unit offers children the opportunity to:
■ explore and develop ideas by using primary and secondary source material as a stimulus for their work
■ use their knowledge and understanding of the behaviour and properties of materials and processes by investigating and combining visual and tactile qualities, and then matching their findings to the purpose of their work
■ evaluate and develop critical skills by using a specialist vocabulary to review, adapt and improve work
■ develop greater knowledge and understanding of the conventions of Indian painting and mask-making by comparing ideas and methods used by craftspeople from different cultures.

ASSESSMENT FOR LEARNING
During this unit, assess children's ability to use primary and secondary source material to develop ideas. By the end of the unit, look for specific evidence to show that children have applied their understanding of the properties of recycled materials, developed knowledge about other artists' work, extended construction techniques and refined their modelling skills. Responses should show they are able to use a specialist vocabulary to evaluate their work, as well as identifying areas for improvement.

▸ **CD-ROM RESOURCES**
■ Presentation: Techniques using recyclable materials and paper laminate Masterclass
■ Resource sheets:
  ■ The *Ramayana* story
  ■ Masks from different cultures
  ■ Comparing masks
  ■ Paintings of the *Ramayana* (1 and 2)
  ■ Looking at paintings of the *Ramayana*
  ■ Characters in the *Ramayana* (1 and 2)
■ Teacher assessment
■ Pupil self-evaluation

SESSION I **EXPLORING FACIAL EXPRESSION IN MASKS**

LEARNING OBJECTIVES

Children will:

- learn to collect visual information by drawing different facial expressions, from direct observation of faces and masks (primary source)

- develop the vocabulary and ability to describe the visual and tactile qualities of masks and explain what they think and feel about them
- develop construction skills by layering paper over a mould to create forms.

VOCABULARY visual and tactile qualities: **line, form, shape, texture, colour, pattern;** masks: **realistic, stylised, decorative, simplified, relief, embossed, contour;** materials: **natural, made, rigid, flexible, pliable, heavy, light**

▼ RESOURCES

- mirrors
- 2B and 4B pencils
- sketchbooks or A2 cartridge paper
- chalk pastels
- A2 black sugar paper
- A4 black sugar paper for testing colours
- selection of small, shallow bowls or saucers
- materials for making a mould – brown paper, crêpe paper, tissue paper, photocopying paper, sugar paper
- petroleum jelly or clingfilm
- non-fungicidal cellulose paste, PVA glue
- thick bristle brushes
- CD-ROM: images of masks from different cultures
- resource sheets: The *Ramayana* story; Masks from different cultures; Comparing masks

ACTIVITY

Explain to pupils that they are going to make a mask of a character from the story of the *Ramayana*. They will collect information in sketchbooks to help develop their ideas at a later date. This session is in three parts and you may wish to teach it over three separate lessons. Explain that in the first part, pupils will investigate facial expression; in the second part, they will explore facial expression in masks from other cultures; and the third part will be a practical activity to learn how to use moulds to make forms.

- During a class discussion, invite pupils to suggest different emotions (make links to PSHE, see Other Areas of Learning, page 70). Give each child a mirror, and ask them to observe and describe to a partner how the shape of face, eyes and cheeks change when they express different emotions, such as happy, sad, astonished, angry, frightened or shocked. Ask the children to look carefully at their eyebrows, the corners of the mouth and the shape of the eyes. Then, either in sketchbooks or on A2 cartridge paper, ask them to observe and draw their own face, depicting four different expressions. They should spend about ten minutes on each drawing.

- Provide masks from different cultures (see the Suppliers list on

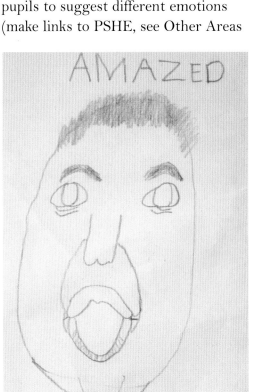

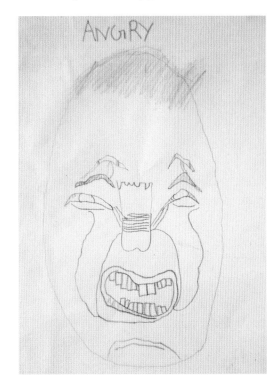

the CD-ROM) or use the **Masks from different cultures** resource sheet. Ask groups of children to discuss the expression on each mask and how this is shown. Make connections with the previous drawing activity – pupils should look at the mouth, cheeks and eyes. Does the decoration on the mask accentuate the expression? Ask them to think about the material the mask is made from, then to feel the contours on the surface of the mask. Ask the groups to fill in the **Comparing masks** resource sheet.

■ Ask pupils to draw the outline of a mask using a yellow pastel on a large piece of black sugar paper (match the shape of the paper to the shape of the mask). Provide A4 black sugar paper for pupils to test their colours. To do this, they should make a small patch of colour and draw a short line next to it, then add another colour on top and draw a short line next to that, and finally blend the two colours with a

finger. Drawing the short lines will remind the children of the ingredients of the original colour they mixed. When they have mixed the colour to their satisfaction, it can be added to their drawing.

■ Provide a selection of small, shallow bowls or saucers for the children to use for moulds, and a variety of papers to experiment with. Show them how to smear the outside of the bowl with petroleum jelly or cover it with cling film. Layer with strips of paper pasted with non-fungicidal cellulose paste. The first layer should be pasted using only water so that it does not stick to the container. If using crêpe paper, the children should use diluted glue (such as PVA adhesive). Cover the bowl with three or four layers of paper. Once the paper laminate is completely dry, the children can gently twist it off the mould. These finished bowls can be used to build forms on the masks (see Session 4).

Can the children:

▶ collect and record relevant information about facial expressions in a limited time?
▶ observe and record the expression, shape, colour, pattern and texture of masks?
▶ confidently apply paper-laminate techniques to create forms using a mould?
▶ describe the visual and tactile qualities of masks using appropriate art vocabulary?

DIFFERENTIATION

Children who have not progressed as far...
Create a word-bank on the interactive whiteboard of vocabulary to describe the masks. When looking at masks, ensure the groups are of mixed ability for language skills. Match pupils with English as an additional language with children with good language skills. Give these pupils concrete experiences to extend their understanding of new vocabulary, such as feeling an embossed surface.

Children who have progressed further...
These pupils could analyse and explain in detail how the features on the mask show expression. Encourage them to make connections with their drawings. Can they make any generalisations from their observations?

SESSION 2 **THE CHARACTERS IN THE** *RAMAYANA*

LEARNING OBJECTIVES

Children will:

- learn to select and collect information through drawing from secondary source material to develop ideas
- develop knowledge and understanding about the conventions of Indian painting
- develop an understanding of the Hindu faith and the significance of the celebration of *Diwali* through exploring the *Ramayana* story.

VOCABULARY form, shape, texture, colour, pattern, composition, flat, profile, stylised, proportion, composition, decoration, ornate, symbolic, perspective

▼ RESOURCES

- ▸ book of the story of the *Ramayana*
- ▸ images of the characters from the *Ramayana* including Sita, Rama and Hanuman, the monkey king (some examples on the CD-ROM)
- ▸ A2 cartridge paper
- ▸ 2B or 4B drawing pencils
- ▸ soft-coloured pencils
- ▸ resource sheets:
  The *Ramayana* story;
  Paintings of the *Ramayana* (1 and 2);
  Looking at paintings of the *Ramayana*;
  Characters in the *Ramayana* (1 and 2)

ACTIVITY

During this session, pupils will be introduced to the story of the *Ramayana*, which may be presented in the context of *Diwali*, the Hindu festival of light, celebrated in the autumn term. Literacy activities (see Other Areas of Learning, page 70) will enable the children to think in depth about the characteristics of the character they have chosen for their mask. If pupils are to write a play of the story, explain that the masks will be used when the play is performed (perhaps to the rest of the school or to another class). You may wish to teach the last activity in a separate lesson.

- Encourage children who celebrate

Diwali to tell the class about what special things they do during the festival, and the significance of the story of the *Ramayana*. If this is not possible, provide information about how and why the Hindu religion celebrates *Diwali* (link with Religious Education – see Other Areas of Learning, page 70).

- Read aloud to the class the story of the *Ramayana*. Next, divide the class into four groups and give each group a colour photocopy of an Indian painting depicting a different scene from the *Ramayana* (using the **Paintings of the Ramayana** resource sheets). Project the questions about Indian paintings

from the **Looking at paintings of the** *Ramayana* resource sheet onto the whiteboard. Ask pupils to look at the paintings in their groups and use the questions as cues for discussion. Choose one person from each group to give feedback to the rest of the class. Keep the discussion open-ended so that others can contribute their own thoughts and feelings.

Encourage a personal response by asking, *Do you like the paintings? Why?* Use questions to further extend the children's thinking – for example: *You have noticed the trees look flat. Do they look as though they are in the distance? Why not?* Focus discussion on the traditional conventions of Indian paintings, such as stylised figures, lack of perspective and symbolism. (Links could also be made to paintings from Ancient Egypt.)

■ Ask each child to select one character from the story. For example:

King Dasharatha – king of Ayodhya; Rama's father

Rama – an incarnation of the God Vishnu

Lakshman – Rama's brother

Sita – Rama's wife

Ravana – the evil ten-headed demon king of Lanka (Sri Lanka)

Hanuman – the general of the monkey army.

For source material, provide good-quality images of the characters from paintings and sculptures illustrated in books and on posters. Some images can be found on the **Characters in the** *Ramayana* resource sheets. Suppliers for posters and other sources can be found on **The** *Ramayana* **story** resource sheet.

■ Ask the children to select a favourite image of the character they have chosen as especially interesting, and to draw the head and headdress of this character. Remind them to draw the details of shape and pattern, paying particular attention to decorative features such as earrings or necklaces. Some pupils may wish to draw their character in profile. When the children have finished their drawings, ask them to add colour using their source image as reference and inspiration.

DIFFERENTIATION

Children who have not progressed as far...
Organise groups of mixed ability in language skills for the discussion. Remind pupils that they should all take turns to speak and they should show respect by listening to each others' opinions. When reading the story, point to illustrations to aid understanding for children with English as a second language.

Children who have progressed further...
Challenge these pupils to draw the demon king Ravana, who has ten heads. The children could work together to collect visual research. Some pupils who celebrate *Diwali* could describe to the rest of the class the significance of *Rangoli* patterns and *diva* lamps. They could also collect information about *Diwali* to make a classroom display or a *PowerPoint* presentation.

SESSION 3 DEVELOPING IDEAS FOR THE DESIGN

LEARNING OBJECTIVES

Children will:

- learn to develop ideas by selecting, sorting and using primary and secondary source material to design a mask for their chosen character
- learn to explore and experiment with the qualities of different materials to develop their own ideas

- learn to use their experience and understanding of the properties of recycled materials to select materials for the structure of their mask
- develop an awareness of different solutions when solving a design problem.

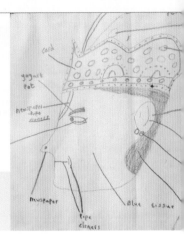

VOCABULARY visual and tactile qualities: **form, shape, texture, colour, pattern;** geometric forms: **cuboid, cylinder, cone, cube, sphere;** materials and processes: **design, construct, structure, recyclable materials**

▼ RESOURCES

- ▶ drawings of expressions and pastel drawings of masks from Session 1
- ▶ drawings of characters in the *Ramayana* from Session 2
- ▶ A2 cartridge paper or sketchbooks
- ▶ 2B or 4B drawing pencils
- ▶ soft coloured pencils
- ▶ recyclable materials for making masks, (modelling card, cardboard tubes, small boxes, yogurt pots, bottle tops, pipe cleaners, metal foil, wire, bendy straws, rubber bands)

ACTIVITY

For this session and the next, it is important you provide pupils with as broad a range of small-scale recyclable materials as possible (see Resources for suggestions). The variety of the selection may affect the quality of the finished mask. It would be useful to establish a class or school recycling bank, if you do not already have one.

■ Explain to the class that during this session they will design a mask of their chosen character from the *Ramayana*. They will use their research, including drawings of their character, their drawings of facial expressions and their learning from looking at masks from other cultures as inspiration to help them develop ideas for their work.

■ Give each child a sheet of A2 cartridge paper and ask them to fold it in half. Explain that they are to draw the face of their chosen character on one half of the paper. Ask them to think about the characteristics of the character they are drawing – for example, *Ravana may be angry*. Focus their attention on their research about facial expressions and how the shape of the mouth and eyes change. Remind them that they may have to accentuate the corners of the mouth and the shape of the eyes. Refer back to the Indian paintings of the *Ramayana* and the importance of stylised shapes, pattern and decoration, particularly on the headdresses. Then ask them to add colour to the design. Remind the children of the richness and brightness

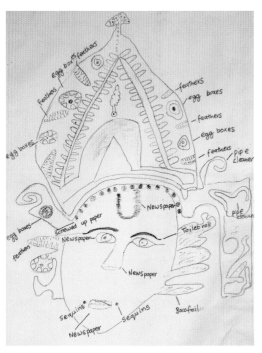

of the colours in the Indian paintings – gold and silver may be added. Ensure they have sufficient time to work on their designs. Encourage pupils to take individual approaches to their design.

■ Explain to the class that they are to use recyclable materials to make the underlying structure of the mask. Provide a range of recyclable materials for pupils to choose from. Discuss with the class the different characteristics of the recyclable and other materials. Compare the flexibility and rigidity of materials and their suitability for different parts of the mask. Ask the children to sort and select the materials they might use and consider how they might need to change them. Encourage them to think about alternative ways of using materials, and share their ideas with a partner. Choose some pupils to talk about their

ideas during a feedback session with the class. Extend the children's thinking by asking, *How can you change the material to make it do what you want?* (for example, twisting newspaper or folding card), or, *Is there a way of combining forms to make them more interesting?* (for example, by building on top of boxes or cylinders)

■ Photocopy the designs for the masks and ask pupils to stick them onto the other half of their sheet of A2 paper. Then ask them to annotate on the photocopy of the drawing how they plan to use recyclable materials to build the underlying structure for the mask.

■ Ask pupils to talk with a partner about why they selected certain materials. Choose some of the children to explain their reasons to the rest of the class.

▼ ASSESSMENT FOR LEARNING

Can the children:
▶ use visual research to develop effective ideas for their mask?
▶ try out materials in new and imaginative ways to develop ideas?
▶ consider the suitability of purpose when selecting materials?
▶ articulate different solutions to a design problem, justifying the choices they make?

DIFFERENTIATION

Children who have not progressed as far...
Give adult support by talking about ways to use materials to extend these children's thinking. Provide lists of words or phrases to help pupils who have difficulty writing to annotate their drawings.

Children who have progressed further...
Challenge these children to work together to make a mask of the ten-headed demon, Ravana, by negotiating tasks, working out how to construct the mask and solving the problem of supporting it. As an alternative, they could make life-size puppets from tissue paper, withies and bamboo canes.

SESSION 4 **BUILDING THE STRUCTURE OF THE MASK**

LEARNING OBJECTIVES

Children will:

■ learn to use their understanding of the behaviour and properties of materials and knowledge of their suitability for different purposes

■ learn to explore and combine the visual qualities of form and space by developing construction and modelling techniques to realise their own ideas

■ reflect and talk about ways to adapt and improve their work as it develops.

VOCABULARY visual and tactile qualities: **form, shape, texture, colour, pattern;** materials and processes: **relief, model, construct, paper laminate, structure, recyclable materials**

▼ RESOURCES

▸ planning sheets
▸ recyclable materials for making masks (modelling card, cardboard tubes, small boxes, yogurt pots, bottle tops, pipe cleaners, metal foil, wire, bendy straws, rubber bands)
▸ moulded forms from Session 1
▸ joining materials (masking tape, PVA glue, glue gun)
▸ materials for making paper laminate – non-fungicidal cellulose paste, water pots, paste brushes or 1-inch decorators' paintbrushes, newspaper, white newsprint
▸ aprons

ACTIVITY

You may wish to teach this session in two parts. First, pupils will construct the underlying framework for the mask; next, they will model the form of the features using paper laminate. It might be useful to make a template for the children to draw around, making sure the holes for the eyes are in the correct place for them to see through. If they are to make a character with a headdress, this should be included as part of the template.

■ Before starting to make the mask, ask pupils if they remember how to build up form using screwed-up newspaper. Show the class how to build up the cheeks, chin, forehead or muzzle for Hanuman, the monkey king, from screwed-up newspaper covered with

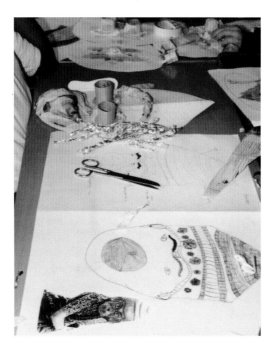

another sheet of newspaper. Remind the children that this has to be joined securely to the base of the mask with masking tape.

■ For the base of the mask, use fairly thick card for strength. Ask pupils to draw around the template, and then cut out the mask and make the holes for the eyes and mouth. They should then follow their plan to construct the features of the character and the headdress from recyclable materials and the forms made from moulds in Session 1. Remind the children to stick seven or eight small pieces of masking tape to the edge of their table before joining their recyclable materials. A glue gun could be used under adult supervision to join awkward shapes.

■ Encourage the class to experiment with materials and change their ideas as they make their mask. Ask the class for their ideas for building up a relief of patterns and shapes (these may include twisting newspaper or using bendy straws, thick cord or string).

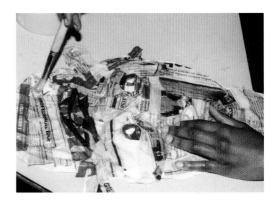

Discuss how these could be attached to the mask.

■ Challenge pupils to describe the process of modelling form with paper laminate. Demonstrate paper-laminate techniques to the class by:

- ■ tearing short strips of newspaper along the grain of the paper
- ■ pasting strips with a non-fungicidal cellulose paste
- ■ modelling form over the basic structure by layering the torn strips of newspaper
- ■ using smaller pieces of torn paper on corners or when modelling the relief patterns
- ■ adding smaller details using tissue paper. Its elasticity makes it useful for filling and it will squash up easily into nodules or bumps for decorative features.

Note: Make the adhesive paste by adding water to a small amount of cellulose paste. Stir continuously to prevent lumps forming until the paste is the consistency of an elastic, free-flowing batter.

■ Show the children how to organise their working area. Provide sheets of newspaper to paste on, as well as stable water pots and thick bristle brushes or painters' brushes to apply the paste. Ensure the paper is fully saturated; wipe off excess glue using the thumb and forefinger. Finally, cover the mask with a layer of white newsprint.

■ Dry the masks away from direct heat. To make sure they do not warp, put large elastic bands around them and they will dry with a very slight curve.

▼ ASSESSMENT FOR LEARNING

Can the children:
▶ make informed choices based on their understanding of materials and match materials to purpose?
▶ show clear intentions, trying out construction techniques and materials in varying ways to explore forms for the underlying structure?
▶ refine modelling techniques by adding details of surface texture and pattern?
▶ identify some ways to improve their work and adapt it independently or with help?

DIFFERENTIATION

Children who have not progressed as far…
Give individual support to pupils lacking technical skills or who experience coordination difficulties. Throughout the making process, refer back to the planning sheet, and focus them on features such as eyebrows or the shape of a moustache. Remind the children of joining techniques – for example, how to cut the bottom of the tube, fan out and flatten (see the Presentation).

Children who have progressed further…
These pupils could design and make their own template for the mask. They could show the class how they have developed alternative ideas for decorative features or give examples of how they have solved problems. Encourage them to refine their work by carefully moulding fine details of pattern and texture using tissue paper (see the Presentation).

SESSION 5 **DECORATING AND EMBELLISHING THE MASK**

LEARNING OBJECTIVES

Children will:

- gain confidence in using colour notes and visual research to embellish their mask
- develop critical skills by evaluating their work, using appropriate vocabulary to describe techniques

- apply developing understanding of tactile and visual qualities of pattern, texture and colour
- compare and comment on ideas and methods used by artists from different times and cultures, making connections with own work.

VOCABULARY visual and tactile qualities: **form, shape, texture, colour, pattern;** colour: **bright/dull, intense, cold/warm, shade, tint, contrast, primary, secondary;** texture: **embossed, relief, surface texture;** pattern: **symmetrical, repeat, regular;** processes: **decorate, embellish;** form: **relief**

▼ RESOURCES

- powder, ready-mixed or block paint in the double primary system: vermillion and crimson; brilliant yellow and lemon yellow; Prussian blue and cobalt blue; plus white and turquoise
- gold and silver paint
- water pots
- mixing palettes
- large, medium and fine bristle brushes
- aprons
- PVA glue and spreaders
- varnish
- materials for decoration (beads, feathers, old jewellery, gold paint, sequins)
- wooden sticks or canes for holding the mask
- masking tape
- resource sheet: Masks from different cultures
- pupil self-evaluation sheet

ACTIVITY

Explain to the class that in this session they will be embellishing and painting their masks, using information about pattern and colour from their research. You may wish to teach these two activities as separate lessons. Make sure the masks are completely dry before painting. Check the surface of the masks before the session – if the print from the newspaper is showing, ask pupils to paint the masks with matt white emulsion paint.

■ Ask the children to organise their working area. Each child should have their own water pot, a mixing palette, thick, medium and fine hog-hair

brushes, fine watercolour brushes and an apron to protect clothing. Show the class a finely painted mask (or image if not available).

■ Ask the class, *What is the logical way to proceed?* Reinforce the sequence for painting. Paint large areas first using a large brush. Make sure an area is completely dry before painting the area adjacent to it, so that colours do not run into each other. Paint lighter colours first. Add fine details of line, shape and pattern using a fine watercolour brush. Remind pupils to wash their brushes well and change their water frequently to ensure clear,

bright colours. Finished masks may be pegged on a washing line across the classroom to dry.

■ When the masks are painted and dry, the sculptures can be varnished with PVA glue or a clear varnish.

■ Ask the children to embellish their mask by gluing beads, pearls and so on to the surface. Encourage them to work from their planning sheets. When the masks are completely dry, carefully and securely attach a wooden stick or cane to the back of the mask with strips of masking tape.

■ Present the class with the masks from different cultures that they first looked at in Session 1 (or use the **Masks from different cultures** resource sheet). Can pupils make connections with their own work? Did they use any of the ideas from other artists in their own work?

■ Ask the children to evaluate their own masks. Which parts do they consider successful? Why? Which parts do they think could be improved? How? What problems did they encounter during the making process? What solutions did they use to overcome them? Challenge them to describe to a partner some of the modelling and construction techniques used to make their masks. Choose one or two children to feed back to the class. Make a word-bank on the whiteboard for pupils to use when they complete their evaluation form.

■ Encourage the children to consider what they have learned during the unit. Which parts did they most enjoy? Why? Ask them whether they have improved their construction and modelling skills. How does their finished mask reflect their original ideas? At this point, the children can fill in the **Pupil self-evaluation** sheet.

▼ ASSESSMENT FOR LEARNING

Can the children:

▶ decorate and embellish their masks working independently from visual research?

▶ imaginatively explore ways to combine the visual qualities to suit their intentions?

▶ evaluate their work using some specialist vocabulary, justifying choices made and identifying areas for improvement?

▶ explain how they have made connections and incorporated ideas from masks from different cultures into their own work?

DIFFERENTIATION

Children who have not progressed as far...
Provide positive support during the painting process, and show these pupils how to hold a brush to paint a fine line. They may require adult support to extend work on decorative features by referring back to their original planning sheet. Encourage them to consider which parts of the mask to decorate.

Children who have progressed further...
These children may require more time to embellish their mask and combine details of pattern, line and shape to accentuate expression, refining their work as it progresses. Ask them to explain to the class how they developed their work by incorporating some ideas from the original masks.

OTHER AREAS OF LEARNING

LITERACY

Read the story of the *Ramayana* to the class, and introduce them to visual references from the British Library website (see the **Looking at paintings of the *Ramayana*** and **Paintings of the *Ramayana*** resource sheets).

Pupils could then:

■ retell the story in their own words or write out favourite scenes

■ write a character analysis of the main personalities, highlighting the themes of good and evil

■ write a play based on some of the events

■ write the dialogue for the action in certain scenes (give individual children different roles, such as writer, director, designer and so on)

■ in pairs, write and illustrate a book on 'How to make a mask'.

DRAMA

■ Using their masks, the class could act out their play of the *Ramayana* for the rest of the school and parents. To develop home/school links, parents could be involved in making costumes and painting scenery and props.

■ The mask-making techniques can be used to depict characters from any story. However, to obtain quality work from pupils, provide stimulating resource material to work from, in order to develop their ideas.

Sculpture

ART AND DESIGN

■ The paper-laminate techniques may be applied in art and design activities – for example, making picture frames, designing and making the head for a puppet, designing an adventure playground, and designing and making musical instruments, such as shakers and drums.

PHYSICAL, SOCIAL AND HEALTH EDUCATION (PSHE)

■ Pupils will gain added respect for the differences between people by learning about the *Ramayana* and *Diwali*. They will develop a deeper understanding and knowledge of celebrations from other cultures.

■ During Session 1, the work on emotions could be extended to include what makes the children happy, sad, angry, frightened and so on. It may be a good time to discuss how to deal with conflict situations in the playground and feelings of anger. The class could discuss different ways of resolving problems through talking.

RELIGIOUS EDUCATION

■ Pupils will develop an understanding of the Hindu faith and the significance of the celebration of *Diwali* through exploring the *Ramayana* story. By looking at Indian paintings of the *Ramayana*, they will understand some of the symbolism and religious beliefs associated with *Diwali*. Other activities – for example, making *Rangoli* patterns, designing cards for *Diwali* and making *diva* lamps, will extend the children's experiences and understanding.

■ *Diva* lamps could be made by using the mould techniques described in Session 1. Decorate with patterns and place a tea light inside.

In art and design, pupils have many opportunities to practise their artistic skills using a range of different media. A computer with appropriate software forms part of this range of media so children should be given the chance to apply their computer skills alongside traditional media. In order to make the most of digital artwork, pupils need to develop their technical as well as creative skills and be offered an array of challenges where they can employ these skills in different art projects.

Prior to Year 4, pupils will have had the opportunity to work with different software and be familiar with the range of digital art tools, including layers. It is anticipated that teachers following this unit will already have some familiarity with the principles of digital software and confidence in teaching ICT processes in general.

The five sessions in this unit are designed to give pupils scope to use digital image-making in different creative contexts. They will apply the skills already acquired in *Art Express* Book 3, but extend understanding of layers using different starting points. They will learn to use different tools for cutting and pasting between images as well as experimenting with filter effects, colour and transparency. Session 1 is similar to Session 1 in *Art Express* Book 3 but is included here to allow pupils to practise, use other tools and consolidate skills. Sessions 2 to 5 are discrete and focus on ideas, with the artistic process itself taking a secondary role.

To complete the work in this unit, you will need image-manipulation software that has layers, such as *Photoshop Elements*, which is a relatively inexpensive yet powerful software package. You can download a trial version of this software from the Adobe website on the internet at www.adobe.com/uk.

AIMS

This unit offers children the opportunity to:

■ record drawings, paintings and work in other media and further develop skills using digital tools and processes

■ experiment with combining digital paint processes with original drawn or painted elements, adding selected photographic elements to create new meanings

■ experiment with scale to create virtual sculptures or to create repeat patterns or motifs for print or textiles

■ develop an understanding of mixed media and the ways in which digital technologies challenge traditional approaches to art and design.

ASSESSMENT FOR LEARNING

The sessions have been designed to enable pupils to practise their skills and extend their knowledge of digital tools and processes. Look for their growing confidence in using and selecting effective tools, and question them about how those tools can be used to create particular outcomes. By the end of the unit, look for evidence of children's increasing confidence with choosing particular tools for modifying and cutting from images related to the art idea. Can pupils use different cutting tools to select all or parts of an image? Can they use filters, colour and transparency options to change the mood and look of an image?

▶ CD-ROM RESOURCES

■ Presentation: Responding to artists; *Photoshop Elements*: Selection tools and layers Masterclass
■ Artworks and images
■ Resource sheets:
  ■ Cutting out a sculpture (1 and 2)
  ■ Site-specific sculpture
  ■ Olympic graphics
  ■ Preparing the container
  ■ Pop portraits (1 and 2)
■ Teacher assessment
■ Pupil self-evaluation

SESSION 1 **COLLAGE – PAST AND PRESENT**

LEARNING OBJECTIVES
Children will:
- develop their creativity by selecting and combining images of the environment, past and present
- develop, practise and consolidate skills and understanding of software tools
- learn to amend and improve their work by editing their image and modifying each layer.

VOCABULARY layer, edit, review, consolidate

▼ RESOURCES

- ▶ computer
- ▶ image-manipulation software with layers (such as *Photoshop Elements*)
- ▶ Presentations:
  Photoshop Elements:
  Selection tools and layers Masterclass;
  Responding to artists Masterclass
- ▶ CD-ROM:
  Demonstration image (Past and Present)

ACTIVITY

In preparation for this session, take a series of photographs of the local environment (school, town or village) and download them into a shared area on the class computer. As an additional activity, you could do this as a separate field trip with the children. To contrast with these modern photographs, search the internet for similar images of the same place during the 1940s and 1950s. The American artist Robert Rauschenberg's images are made up of fragments of popular press images. Search again on the internet to find examples of his work and bookmark the website(s) for later use with pupils. Finally, familiarise yourself with the Presentation and the demonstration image on the CD-ROM.

■ Use the interactive whiteboard to show the children where the digital resources are stored on the computer. Talk to pupils about creating a digital collage using fragments of images of the local environment, past and present. Show them the work of Robert Rauschenberg and the way in which he used fragments of images taken from contemporary newspapers to create his collages. Discuss the mood, form, content and process of his screen prints. Explain that the collage they will create will use digital images from the local environment, past and present, using the Rectangular tool and the Lasso tool.

■ Demonstrate how to open a new blank A4 page (see the Presentation). This will be the background for the collage and is similar to giving out sheets of paper for drawing. (See the Presentation for tips on how to set the paper size.)

■ Using the interactive whiteboard, demonstrate how to open an image from the local environment. Explain that this first image will be the one onto which the other images will be layered. Show the children how to use the Rectangular selection tool to choose a section of the image. Using the Move tool, drag the selected section onto the blank A4 sheet. With the Move tool still selected, drag the corner of the image until it fills the A4 sheet. Invite pupils to do the same and save the image.

■ Again using the interactive whiteboard, demonstrate how to choose a second image and cut a section from it. Talk to the children about the content of the image and the importance of choosing a section that shows an interesting building or landmark. Use the Move tool to drag this second section onto the first image. Again use the Move tool to change the size of the selection. Invite pupils to do the same and then save the image to add the new section to the saved file. Repeat the process until there are three fragments layered onto the original background image.

■ Show the children the Lasso tool and demonstrate how this allows you to cut an irregular shape from an image in the same way as the Rectangular tool. Invite pupils to add three more layers using the Lasso tool. Save the image.

■ Show pupils how to edit the layers using the process described in Session 3 of the digital media unit in *Art Express* Book 3. Save this final image and print.

■ In a plenary session, invite the children to summarise what they have learned and to recap on their newly acquired skills.

ASSESSMENT FOR LEARNING

Can the children:
▶ create a digital collage that successfully combines different images?
▶ use their existing knowledge of software tools with confidence?
▶ change and improve their collage using tools purposefully?

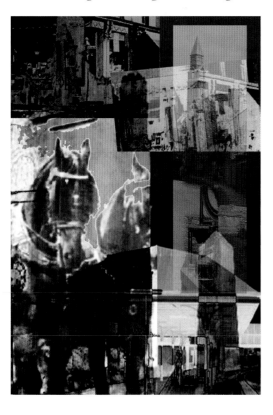

DIFFERENTIATION

Children who have not progressed as far...
For some pupils, it may be helpful to work in carefully selected pairs so they can help each other. The task could also be modified so that children only use one layer.

Children who have progressed further...
Some pupils may already be familiar with certain processes and be able to use the computer tools creatively to produce their own design using layers. It may be helpful to group pupils with prior knowledge of software so they can support each other in extending their experiments and understanding.

SESSION 2 **SCULPTURE IN PLACE**

LEARNING OBJECTIVES

Children will:

- learn to select and use photographs in their work
- develop their imagination by considering and placing their own sculpture in an environment

- learn more about sculpture as a feature in the environment.

VOCABULARY virtual

▼ **RESOURCES**

▸ photographs of the school environment or other locations
▸ computer
▸ image-manipulation software with layers (such as *Photoshop Elements*)
▸ Presentation: *Photoshop Elements*: Selection tools and layers Masterclass
▸ resource sheets: Cutting out a sculpture (1 and 2); Site-specific sculpture

▼ **ASSESSMENT FOR LEARNING**

Can the children:

▸ use a digital camera to photograph their sculpture?
▸ use digital photographs to place their sculpture effectively in a new virtual environment?
▸ talk about the way sculpture is located in the environment?

ACTIVITY

During this session, pupils will use image-manipulation software to place a photograph of a sculpture in a chosen location, as well as explore scale and composition. Before the session, take photographs of the school environment and ask the children to find images of famous places on the internet (for example, Trafalgar Square). Ask pupils to photograph a sculpture of their own (made in an art lesson) against a green background (see the **Green screen** resource sheet in *Art Express* Book 3). Alternatively, the children could create one using natural forms, such as stones, bark or shells. Look at the **Cutting out a sculpture** resource sheets to revise features of the green-screen process, use of the Magic wand and other tools. See also the Presentation on the CD-ROM.

■ Open the **Site-specific sculpture** resource sheet using the interactive whiteboard and click on the links to show pupils sculptures in various settings; discuss the artists' work.

■ Show the children where the photographs of famous locations are stored. Select and open an image as a background location for the sculpture. Now open an image of a child's sculpture and demonstrate how to select the green background using the Magic wand tool. Drag the sculpture onto the background image. Invite pupils to do the same. Save the image.

■ Demonstrate how to change the scale of the sculpture. Ask pupils to experiment with changing the scale of their own sculpture to suit the background location. Save the image.

■ Show the children how to change the colour of the sculpture, and how to adjust its brightness and contrast to suit the lighting conditions of the background image. Save the image.

■ Use the interactive whiteboard to share individual outcomes. Discuss the chosen locations of the sculptures, and the ways in which pupils have transformed their sculptures to match the requirements of each location.

DIFFERENTIATION

Children who have not progressed as far...
For some pupils, it may be helpful to work in carefully selected pairs so that they can help each other.

Children who have progressed further...
It might be helpful to group pupils with prior knowledge of software so they can support one another in extending experiments. Invite them to take further photographs of ordinary objects and change them into sculptures in the environment, perhaps inspired by work from the **Site-specific sculpture** resource sheet.

SESSION 3 **OLYMPIC CONTAINERS**

LEARNING OBJECTIVES
Children will:
- develop their imagination by creating a contemporary vase or plate based on Greek designs
- develop an understanding of the design of Greek vases and plates.

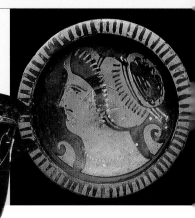

VOCABULARY Olympic, mythological, symbol, containers

ACTIVITY

In this session, pupils will modify an image of a Greek container by adding graphic symbols representing modern Olympic sports. Greek vases and plates are made of red terracotta clay with a black design, often commemorating sporting, historic or mythological events. Before the session, look at and discuss the style and purpose of Greek containers with the children. Search the internet for images of containers, contemporary Olympic pictograms and sport images. You can use the **Olympic graphics** resource sheet with pupils to find and explore sporting symbols. Save your chosen images to the computer. Have the container images ready, as described in the **Preparing the container** resource sheet.

- Show the children the images of Greek containers (see the CD-ROM) and discuss their design and original purpose. Talk about the Olympics and how the modern Olympics are descended from the games that began in the city of Olympia in Ancient Greece. Explain that the class will decorate a traditional Greek container using modern sporting symbols to link the past and present.

- Using the interactive whiteboard, demonstrate how to open a new blank A4 page. Open a Greek container image and copy and paste it onto the page. Scale it so that it fills the page. Ask the children to do the same and then save the image.

- Demonstrate how to open one of the sport symbols. Use the Magic wand tool (see the Presentation) to select the background of the symbol, then inverse the selection to select the symbol itself. Use the Move tool to drag the symbol onto the image of the Greek container and scale it to suit the outline and dimensions of the pot. Save the image. Ask pupils to do the same on their own container, repeating the process to add on several symbols.

- Use the interactive whiteboard to share individual outcomes and discuss the differences between the children's containers and the Greek designs.

RESOURCES

- computer
- image-manipulation software with layers (such as *Photoshop Elements*)
- Presentations: *Photoshop Elements*: Selection tools and layers Masterclass; Responding to artists Masterclass
- CD-ROM: Demonstration images (1–4); images of Greek vases and plates
- resource sheets: Olympic graphics; Preparing the container

ASSESSMENT FOR LEARNING

Can the children:
- use image-manipulation software to create an original design for a Greek container?
- talk about their designs and how they are similar to, and different from, traditional Greek vases?

DIFFERENTIATION

Children who have not progressed as far...
It may be helpful for some children to be paired so that they can support each other in modifying their image.

Children who have progressed further...
Pupils who understand the process of cutting and pasting between images could demonstrate to the class using the interactive whiteboard. They might also be able to draw their own figures on the containers, using the Brush tool. It may be useful to identify a few children to act as troubleshooters to support others.

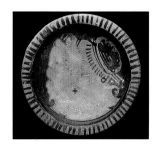

SESSION 4 POP PORTRAITS

LEARNING OBJECTIVES

Children will:

- develop their creativity by selecting appropriate source images and colours, leading to a controlled and effective image
- develop practical skills by using digital software with purpose and deliberation to simplify and stylise a portrait

- learn about the work of pop artists and, in particular, Andy Warhol.

VOCABULARY Andy Warhol, screen print, pop art, virtual

▼ RESOURCES

- ▶ computer
- ▶ image-manipulation software with layers (such as *Photoshop Elements*)
- ▶ printer
- ▶ resource sheet: Pop portraits (1 and 2)

ACTIVITY

In this session, children will create a pop portrait using the work of Andy Warhol as a starting point. In preparation for the session, take portrait photographs of the children and download them onto the computer.

■ Use the interactive whiteboard to show children the work of Andy Warhol on the internet. Talk about the pop art movement that started in Britain during the 1950s. Explain that some of the best work was created by Andy Warhol in New York during the 1960s. Engage the children in a discussion about pop art. Talk about different printing processes and the impact of screen printing, in the style of Warhol. There is an animation showing the Warhol process at www.warhol.org/interactive/silkscreen/main.html (click on the link at the bottom right of the screen).

■ On the same webpage there is a link (at the bottom left) to a virtual screen-printing process. Using the interactive whiteboard, follow the on-screen instructions to create your own virtual screen print. Discuss the process of creating the image with the children. Encourage them to try out the process individually at a later stage.

■ Using the interactive whiteboard, demonstrate how to create a new blank A4 page. Show the children where

their portrait images are stored and then open an image to use for the demonstration. Explain that they are going to create their own Andy Warhol self-portrait using image-manipulation software.

■ Demonstrate how to copy the portrait image and paste it onto the new blank page. Scale the portrait so that it fits the page. Invite the children to do the same and save the image.

■ Using the interactive whiteboard, show children the Layer palette. It should show two layers – a blank image and their portrait. Demonstrate how to create a new transparent layer by going to the Layer drop-down menu and choosing New Layer. You should now see three layers in the Layer palette. Ask the children to do the same and save the image.

■ In the Layer palette, make a new blank layer. Choose the Pencil tool and trace the main shapes onto the blank layer (see the **Pop portraits** resource sheets). Save your image.

■ Switch off the layer (click on the eye in the Layer palette) that contains your photograph and save the image again.

■ Use the Paint Bucket tool to colour the drawn outline and save the image.

■ In the Layer palette, select the original portrait image. Right-click the mouse and choose Duplicate Layer. Click on the duplicate portrait layer and drag it onto the Layer palette.

■ Make sure the duplicate portrait image is selected and remove all the colour by selecting Adjust Colour, and then Remove Colour from the Enhance

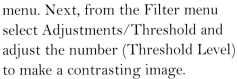

menu. Next, from the Filter menu select Adjustments/Threshold and adjust the number (Threshold Level) to make a contrasting image.

■ Finally, use the Magic wand to select the white parts of the portrait image and press Delete to remove these. Save the image.

■ Print the images and hold a class discussion on the portraits the children have created, and how they compare to the style of Andy Warhol.

▼ **ASSESSMENT FOR LEARNING**

Can the children:
▶ create a successful image with a careful choice of colour?
▶ use appropriate tools to simplify their image?
▶ create a portrait in the style of Andy Warhol?

DIFFERENTIATION

Children who have not progressed as far…
These pupils may need additional help with drawing the outline portrait and changing the colour of their photograph.

Children who have progressed further…
Pupils who understand the process of creating a simplified image could create several colour variations of their image, as Andy Warhol would have done. Some of these children could support other pupils in completing their work.

SESSION 5 **STILL LIFE**

LEARNING OBJECTIVES
Children will:
- gain confidence in their ability to use digital software creatively to realise their ideas
- learn to improve their work by considering the qualities they see in their own and others' work
- learn about the ways in which artists create still-life paintings.

VOCABULARY still life, collage, genre

▼ RESOURCES

- ▸ computer
- ▸ image-manipulation software with layers (for example, *Photoshop Elements*)
- ▸ printer
- ▸ Presentation: *Photoshop Elements*: Selection tools and layers Masterclass
- ▸ CD-ROM: images of still-life objects and children's still-life compositions
- ▸ an excellent internet site for famous images: http://commons.wikimedia. org/wiki/Category:Still_life _paintings
- ▸ pupil self-evaluation sheet

ACTIVITY

This activity challenges pupils to look at still-life paintings by a variety of artists and to create a digital still life of their own, using a selection of still-life objects.

In preparation for this activity, search on the internet for still-life paintings by artists such as Picasso, Braque and Cézanne, and bookmark the pages. Print a copy of each still life and create a display in the classroom for visual reference.

It would be beneficial if this activity followed a traditional art activity, where the children have made a drawing or painting of a still life from first-hand observation.

■ Show the children the images of still-life paintings by different artists. Talk to them about the composition and style of the work. Works by some artists, such as Picasso and Braque, are abstract, while others, such as those by Cézanne or some of the Dutch still-life genre painters, are more realistic. Talk about the arrangement of objects, fruit or vegetables, the different kinds of surface and the backgrounds in the artists' work. Explain to the children that they are going to create their own still life, making a selection from different still-life elements to create an original design.

■ Demonstrate how to create a new blank A4 page and talk to the children about the different still-life elements

ASSESSMENT FOR LEARNING

Can the children:
- create an effective still-life collage using image-manipulation software?
- describe the process of creating a collage and express their feelings about their own work as well as the work of artists?
- recognise different types of still-life painting?

they can choose from to create their image. First, pick one of the table images from the CD-ROM. Next, use the Magic wand tool to select the background of the picture. Go to the Select menu and inverse the selection. Then use the Move tool to drag the table onto the A4 background. Ask pupils to do the same. Save the image.

■ Choose a background fabric from the CD-ROM and demonstrate how to open this second image. Cut this out from the background and arrange it behind the table image. Save the image.

■ Repeat the process, adding new elements to the still life to build the composition. Refer the children to the still-life display in the classroom to give them inspiration. Remind them to save at regular intervals.

■ Review the layers, changing the scale of objects to create the most interesting composition. Demonstrate

how to use the Hue/Saturation menu to change the colour of a layer (see the Presentation on the CD-ROM).

■ Print and display the children's images alongside the artists' still lifes. In a plenary, compare and contrast the children's and artists' work.

■ At the end of this final session, provide each child with a **Pupil self-evaluation** sheet for feedback on the work undertaken throughout the unit.

DIFFERENTIATION

Children who have not progressed as far…
It may be helpful to pair some pupils carefully so that they can help each other. Additional support may be needed for children who experience difficulty in selecting the right tools to create their collage.

Children who have progressed further…
Some children may show a willingness to explore different tools and describe what they do. Encourage them to reflect this in their work, showing greater technical control, perhaps by applying filter effects to add texture to some of the objects in their still life.

OTHER AREAS OF LEARNING

ART AND DESIGN

- Children can use a range of computer tools to create imaginative pictures that can be used to develop storybooks with moving parts.

LITERACY

- Digital collage can be used to develop imaginary images based on poems, plays or stories read in class.

GEOGRAPHY

- Pupils could draw up annotated plans using an appropriate software package to redesign their classroom, outdoor spaces or other areas around the school.
- A range of digital processes can be used to explore ways of improving the look of local environments such as local swimming amenities, the high street, the local park, or railway station.

Digital media

ICT

- Children can use digital processes to combine drawn, scanned and photographic images to communicate ideas: for example, in a *PowerPoint* presentation.

HISTORY

- Children can create images using digital media and research using the library and the internet to imagine how the school environment – classrooms, uniforms, or wartime features such as propaganda posters – might have looked during the 1940s.

PHYSICAL, SOCIAL AND HEALTH EDUCATION (PSHE)

- Children can create a digital collage using images from newspapers and other media to comment on a recent local, national or international event.